Pastor Gregg gives some truly powerful insights on a topic of great importance: finding God's will. Who among us wouldn't enjoy a greater understanding of God's plan for our lives? This book sets forth principles that will help anyone wrestling with this challenging subject. God has spoken to my life through Pastor Gregg on many occasions, and He has done so again through this book.

LANCE BERKMAN
All-Star Major League Baseball Player

Many men can write a book, but few can live the life they write. *Finding God's Will* is Gregg Matte. It's wise, it's easy, and it works. I've never known a better man or read a better book.

JOHN R. BISAGNO
Pastor Emeritus, Houston's First Baptist Church, Houston, Texas

Sin duda este libro será de bendición para el lector y le ayudara a identificar su llamado y su destino en Dios. El mensaje que Gregg comunica es de manera relevante, impactante y practico, es una persona que vive lo que predica y es una persona que forma cambios positivos en el Reino de Dios. Yo soy testigo de lo que Dios esta haciendo por medio de Gregg y sin duda entiende el llamado de Dios en su vida. Sé que sus predicaciones han marcado la vida de miles y lo seguirá haciendo. Me siento muy privilegiado de ser parte de lo que Gregg esta haciendo por medio del mundo.

VÍCTOR J. CÁRDENAS
Founder of Otra Onda Inc. and Vocalist of Zona 7

Gregg Matte, with rare grace, candor and biblical accuracy, has taken us on a much-needed journey to find satisfying answers to the questions of God's role in the pain and joy that accompanies the life of every follower of Christ.

MATT CARTER
Lead Pastor, The Austin Stone Community Church, Austin, Texas

Gregg Matte speaks clearly into the confusion of so many followers of Jesus who aren't sure how to follow Him. With a shepherd's passion and practical wisdom, Gregg has provided a timeless resource for finding God's will.

DR. LARRY CRABB
Author of 66 *Love Letters*, founder and director of NewWay Ministries

"God, why are you allowing this to happen?" It is a question that we all ask but rarely understand. *Finding God's Will* can help you understand how God works your life for His purpose. But this isn't just some manual. Gregg uses humor along with humility to speak to our hearts. *Finding God's Will* made me feel as if Gregg were sitting right next to me while he explained the unexplainable.

MORGAN ENSBERG
Former All-Star Major League Baseball Player

From among all of the voices offering guidance along life's journey, to whom will you choose to listen? I frequently listen to my friend Gregg Matte. Gregg is qualified to speak because he has faithfully and consistently chosen to listen to the one supreme wise voice—the same voice who spoke to Moses through a burning bush and guided his steps with pillars of fire and smoke. You are sure to enjoy this journey into a deeper understanding of discerning the will of God.

DR. BRIAN G. FISHER
Senior Pastor, Grace Bible Church, College Station, Texas

I can't think of anyone better to help university students and young adults (okay, anybody!) discover their role in God's story than my friend Gregg Matte. *Finding God's Will* is practical and powerful fuel for a life that counts for what matters most.

LOUIE GIGLIO
Founder, The Passion Movement, Passion City Church, Atlanta, Georgia

People today value authenticity. Gregg Matte's thoughts on finding God's will for our lives are a true resource for wisdom and encouragement along this journey.

STEVE M. LIVINGSTON, ED. D
Head of School, Houston Christian High School, Houston, Texas

How could Gregg Matte have known when he started the Breakaway Ministry at Texas A&M University as a 19-year-old college student that he was walking in God's perfect will for his life? God was preparing him at that time to one day become the pastor of Houston's First Baptist Church. Gregg's book shows that when we seek God with our whole heart, it is impossible to get out of His will. You will love the transparency with which Gregg writes about his own experiences. What a blessing to know Gregg Matte and to call him Pastor.

CAROLE LEWIS
National Director, First Place 4 Health

I have known Pastor Matte for many years and have seen his determination to make this world a better place. As you read the pages of his book, you will find yourself motivated and inspired not only to discover God's will for your own life but also to reach out and give the hope of our Lord to those around us daily.

DRAYTON MCLANE
Chairman and CEO, Houston Astros

I'm thrilled to recommend my pastor's book to you! The style that makes him so well loved at the podium also flows from his pen. Gregg Matte is a great Bible teacher, and no one can illustrate a point more masterfully. Not many people fall asleep at my church. You're about to find out why. Enjoy! The God of God's will awaits you.

BETH MOORE
Bestselling author and founder of Living Proof Ministries

I couldn't put it down! This book is packed with truth to help answer the question that every believer asks. Gregg shares gripping stories, both personal and biblical, that speak to finding God's will in every season of life!

CHRISTY NOCKELS
Songwriter and worship leader for Passion Conferences

Finally, Gregg Matte has written a book! Gregg has lived and breathed these truths. How do we discern the will of God? How do we live a life that matters? The answers are found here!

BEN STUART
Director, Breakaway Ministries, College Station, Texas

If you are looking for the will of God, you have to find it through your own personal encounter with God; but if you are looking for a methodology that will get you there every time, Gregg Matte has provided your guide for finding it. Instead of using secular principles, however, he has given his readers a way to accomplish this task based on the Word of God. I strongly encourage everyone to read this book.

PAIGE PATTERSON
President, Southwestern Baptist Theological Seminary, Forth Worth, Texas

Gregg really hits a home run here. Skillfully blending Scripture and story, he shows us that God's will is less about finding hidden treasure and much more about a path daily walked in communion with and submission to our Lord. It is in that daily journey that God's will finds us.

JASON POST
Church planter and pastor, WorldVenture, Ireland

Having known Gregg Matte since his teen years, I have watched this man literally grow up through the truths in this book. Gregg's personal life examples only magnify his desire to find, follow and communicate the heart and will of God. Through this book, he has found yet another means to spur more of us in that same pursuit.

CHRIS RICE
Songwriter

Gregg Matte has written a wonderful book for young and old alike on finding God's will. Pastor Matte's insights not only come from his sound and thoughtful interpretations of Scripture but also emerge from the fires of his own experiences of seeing and enduring the troubles of this life. I highly recommend this engaging book as a helpful resource for cultivating the wisdom we all need for following God's will.

DR. ROBERT SLOAN
President, Houston Baptist University, Houston, Texas

When it comes to understanding God's will, Gregg Matte is more than a theological theorist; he is also a season practitioner who has captured the essence of this vital pursuit through in depth study of God's Word and his own obedience. Finding God's Will is a must-read for all Christians who want a better grasp on clear direction from the Father.

STEVE STROOPE
Lead pastor, Lake Pointe Church, Rockwall, Texas

FINDING GOD'S WILL

Seek Him, Know Him, Take the Next Step

GREGG MATTE

Regal

From Gospel Light
Ventura, California, U.S.A.

Published by Regal
From Gospel Light
Ventura, California, U.S.A.
www.regalbooks.com
Printed in the U.S.A.

Library of Congress Cataloging-in-Publication Data
Matte, Gregg.
Finding God's will : seek him, know him, take the next step / Gregg Matte.
p. cm.
ISBN 978-0-8307-5658-2 (hardcover)
1. God—Will. 2. Providence and government of God—Christianity. I. Title.
BT135.M36 2010
248—dc22
2010029909

1 2 3 4 5 6 7 8 9 10 11 12 13 14 15 / 20 19 18 17 16 15 14 13 12 11 10

Rights for publishing this book outside the U.S.A. or in non-English languages are
administered by Gospel Light Worldwide, an international not-for-profit ministry.
For additional information, please visit www.glww.org, email info@glww.org, or write
to Gospel Light Worldwide, 1957 Eastman Avenue, Ventura, CA 93003, U.S.A.

To order copies of this book and other Regal products in bulk quantities,
please contact us at 1-800-446-7735.

Dedicated to Greyson and Valerie.

The life ahead of you will have many ups and downs;
but through it all, you can rest, knowing both your earthly
father and your heavenly Father love you and desire the best for you.
May knowing God be your life's quest, and finding
His will your most satisfying reward.

CONTENTS

ACKNOWLEDGMENTS

My gratitude extends to the people of Houston's First Baptist Church. It is impossible to out love you! You are a blessing to my family and my walk with the Lord. What a gift to lead such a great body of believers. Our heritage is rich and our future bright as we continue to live as a "relevant biblical community" in our city.

To the staff of Houston's First Baptist Church: It is compelling to be surrounded by such godly, effective and excellent people. You challenge me to bring my A-game each day as we serve together. What a joy!

My family and friends: The fact that I am fully known and fully loved with you creates a safe place in my life. Thank you for your prayers and encouragement.

Muchas gracias to Leigh McElroy, a wonderful editor. Your efforts were beyond valuable. Thank you for working as if this was your book instead of mine. You are a gifted writer and used of the Lord.

Thanks to Carole Lewis for connecting me with Regal publishing, and thanks to Regal for partnering with me on this project. This book would still be thoughts in my journal without your vision of publishing. I'm grateful.

Thank you to my assistants, Joanna Cooke and Mary Smith. I appreciate your hard work on this project and keeping my life in order. You are both a blessing, and I'm so grateful to have such a committed dynamic duo in my office.

To the smartest folks in the room, my research team, I say εὐχαριστία (for the rest of us, that's "thanks" in Greek). You are tremendously gifted intellectually and use it for the Lord. I'm grateful for your study and service to the Body of Christ by your aid in my research.

Years of gratitude to Kelly, the greatest fruit of God's will in my life. Your endless encouragement and wisdom have blessed me. Often I'm the one with the microphone or author's pen and, therefore, receive the accolades, but it is you who will have the crowns in heaven. Thank you for listening to me preach literally thousands of messages, and you still smile and take notes. Thank you for never once discouraging me as I glared at the screen of the laptop, saying, "I'll be there in a minute. I'm working on the book." You are the best mom and wife imaginable.

Most importantly, thank You, Jesus. Your will in my life is far more than I ever imagined or deserved. You have taken me a mighty long way, and I look forward to the next burning bush You place before me. "Here I am!"

WANDERING AND WONDERING

The tables were perfectly arranged, each with a clever "freebie" designed to entice soon-to-be college grads to stop and chat. Handsome men and pretty women stood nearby dressed to the nines and ready to answer questions about employment opportunities with their respective employers. Unfortunately, I had forgotten the date of the annual business school career fair and was clad in my regular undergraduate uniform: shorts, a collared shirt and a bulging backpack.

"Aren't you going home to put on a suit?" one of my friends asked as we wound our way through the maze. I wasn't sure if I should answer no and leave it at that, or tell him that I didn't even own a suit. Unfortunately, I'd forgotten about the one day out of four years that I should have at least put on long pants—and my grades weren't likely to compensate for my underdressed appearance.

Despite sporting a new standard for "business casual," I walked the walk, talked the talk and crammed highlighters with company logos into my bag, looking more like a pen thief than a would-be young executive.

The most important days of life can sneak up on you, and more than once I've arrived at a significant intersection unprepared and unassuming. I met my wife, for example, while I was putting mustard on a hamburger at a party. I only went there because I was hungry. Thankfully, that story ended well. Others have gone south rather quickly. I wasn't feeling too optimistic that day at the business school career fair. *Is this it?* I wondered. *Is life just a sea of tables with a gimmick or two thrown in?*

I'd hoped for something more compelling (and convincing) than that corporate labyrinth . . . maybe a neon light blinking around the right company logo, or some other clear sign telling me which way to go. How was I to know God's directing? Which path was I supposed to choose? Like most of my classmates, I was looking for a place to spend 40-plus hours a week, preferably with a nice office and interesting work to talk about with inquiring friends and relatives. I wanted to be a team player and, of course, make some money, but nothing I saw that day stirred my heart. I dutifully gathered up pieces of marketing collateral, but mostly I "wondered as I wandered." How would I make the right decision? Did a job exist that matched my desires with God's will? If it did, would I know it when I saw it?

My half-hearted search at the career fair paralyzed more than energized me. That day my 22-year-old heart realized there must be something more. I knew I was made to fulfill a plan, but the immediate path I was supposed to take was not clear to me at all. Maybe you've been in a similar situation (although you were probably better dressed). If you've wandered among a confusing jumble of choices, wondering what turn to take—

deeply sensing that your decision would ultimately define you, and fearful of making a mistake—then this book is for you.

Join me on a journey to discover the will of God. The journey begins at a burning bush with a man named Moses for a guide. It demonstrates that there is a plan, a path and a divine purpose for each one of us. That afternoon job fair marked the day my meandering began to morph into a mission. I didn't find a job, but I did find a direction. I knew it was God's "table" I was looking for—and His work I longed to do 365 days a year for the rest of my life. I wanted to know His will, even if I wasn't exactly ready to do it. I wanted to move in the direction He had planned for me. I still do. Because knowing His will is like the advantage of having the biggest, toughest kid on your dodge ball team. Ultimate victory is assured, even when you get pegged with the ball.

I've found that the best place to begin to know God's will is in His Word. One place I've returned over and over again is to the book of Exodus, and the story of Moses. In fact, in the margin of my Bible, next to Exodus 3, I've written these words: "The process of the call to Houston's First Baptist Church." This is the Scripture my wife, Kelly, and I pored over as we sought the will of God in leaving a thriving student ministry we'd founded and nurtured in a small college town to pastor a church in Houston, Texas. Vocational ministry, as you can imagine, didn't have a table at that career fair. Thankfully, I'm 110 percent sure I took the right path and followed God's leading. I pray the following pages will help you do the same.

If you were to come into my office today and say, "Pastor, I don't know what God's will is for my life," I would invite you to sit down and turn with me to Exodus and examine the life of Moses.

"Well," you might say, "I'm not so interested in that Moses guy. What I *really* need to know is whether to take this job, or marry this girl, or how to raise these kids." I understand. I do. Those looming life decisions can press in hard on our hearts and give us a sense of overwhelming urgency. I've felt the weight of them too. But I've learned from experience that knowing God's will helps me to know Him—and knowing Him helps me to know His will. Moses learned this long before me, so his experience is instructive. He became caught up in a lifelong process of discovery—kind of an endless loop—of knowing God and knowing His will, knowing God and knowing His will. This, my friend, is the loop of a lifetime! So get on and keep going. Discover the on-ramps and close the exits. By the end you'll have realized the pleasure of knowing God, and as a result, you'll discover the joy and satisfaction that come from knowing His will for you.

1

FROM FAR SIDE
TO FIRST STEP

Moses' experience of discovering God's will began rather late in his life, and in the middle of nowhere. At the time of Moses' birth, the Egyptian pharaoh was murdering young Hebrew boys because he feared losing his power to the growing number of Israelite slaves. Moses' mother saved her son's life by placing him in the river in a basket, where Pharaoh's daughter rescued him. The name "Moses" actually means "saved from the water."[1] He grew up in the palaces of Egypt, but as a young man he committed murder, killing an Egyptian he saw mistreating one of his fellow Israelites. Guilty and on the run, he wound up in the land of Midian, tending his father-in-law's sheep—and he remained in that humble job for 40 years! Once protected, privileged and seemingly destined for greatness, Moses turned 80 in obscurity, with few accomplishments to his credit.

But one day, everything changed. On the far side of the mountain, at an age when Moses might have believed nothing new or surprising could happen to him, God called him to his life's mission:

Now Moses was tending the flock of Jethro his father-in-law, the priest of Midian, and he led the flock to the far side of the desert and came to Horeb, the mountain of God. There the angel of the LORD appeared to him in flames of fire from within a bush. Moses saw that though the bush was on fire it did not burn up. So Moses thought, "I will go over and see this strange sight—why the bush does not burn up." When the LORD saw that he had gone over to look, God called to him from within the bush, "Moses! Moses!" And Moses said "Here I am" (Exod. 3:1-4).

At this point in his life, Moses was an unlikely candidate for a major assignment. He was old. He had made some major mistakes. He was stuck in the middle of nowhere, working in the same low-profile job he'd held for four decades. He was on the far side of the mountain, but he was about to be brought face to face with the mountain maker!

You are never too old, too young, too remote or too ruined for God to use you. Senior adults, you're needed. You're vital to the mission of the church. You're loved, wanted, respected. Don't check out or lose interest. Students, you're mission-critical too. The future of the church depends upon your continuing growth and faithfulness. Don't think you can wait to contribute or serve. And for those of you who've made mistakes that keep you clinging to the sidelines in fear and shame, you are not excluded from getting back on the path of God's will. Someone whose life has been marked by greed can become a giver. A person with a promiscuous past can still have a godly marriage that blesses and inspires others. God specializes in fresh starts.

How do I know? Look at God's Word. If His will is reserved for the perfect, then tear out the 13 books of the Bible written by the apostle Paul, the psalms of David and the wisdom of Solomon. Disregard the patriarchs and the leaders of the Early Church. After all, Abraham lied, Jacob cheated, David had an affair, Moses murdered; Rahab was a harlot, Paul was a persecutor of Christians, and Timothy was afraid and sickly. Even Peter had plenty of egg on his face, and he walked more closely with Jesus than just about anyone!

But if God's will shines even brighter in the redemption of the fallen (and it does!), then keep your Bible just as it is, and let it teach you that you are not alone. In fact, you are in good company. And you are a perfect candidate for God to use, in spite of where you are and what you've done or failed to do.

To Find God's Will, Do God's Will

We know where Moses was when God called to him. We know how old he was and what his past held. But maybe more important than any of these things is what Moses was doing when he encountered the burning bush: *nothing remarkable*. He was tending his father-in-law's flock, like he'd done every day for half his life or more. Shepherding was his regular routine, and he was faithfully doing his job. Leading the flock to this area of the mountain was undoubtedly not a special occasion for Moses but something he did regularly, for shepherds often moved their flocks as the seasons changed and grazing conditions varied. He had almost certainly been on the backside of this mountain before.

Did you notice that he didn't even have his own sheep? They belonged to his father-in-law. Nothing remarkable there, for sure. He is on the backside of a mountain, watching someone else's flock. But somehow he is ripe for God's choosing. God is not looking to elevate the already elevated. He is looking to tell a story—a story of the greatness of His plan, not a story about our skill. The stage is being set. This is going to be a day of unexpected change. The hinge is about to swing on the "before" and "after" of Moses' life.

Today could be that same kind of day for you. This week, a relational intersection could change the course of your life. A conversation on bended knee could be the tipping point of your prayer life. By the same token, an unexpected phone call could bring you to your knees in grief. Life isn't always easy. Its course can change in seconds, even as we try to plan out the years. What Jesus said in Matthew 6:34 is true: "Do not worry about tomorrow, for tomorrow will worry about itself. Each day has enough trouble of its own."

Often we imagine that God's will is "out there" somewhere, 90 miles ahead of us and hidden like a needle in a haystack. But for Moses, it was very close, and not hidden at all. Each step tending his father-in-law's sheep in Nowheresville was a step closer to discovery. In fact, God helped him see it by calling attention to it, just in case he might have passed it by. He caused an ordinary bush to burn in an attention-getting way and appeared to Moses within the flame, calling him by name.

You might say, "I'd stop, too, if I saw a little self-starting bonfire like that, or if I heard God audibly speak my name." But would you, like Moses, be faithful in doing the thing that God has put before you to do when He called?

The best way to *find* the will of God is to *do* the will of God. Let me offer an example to bring this home. How do you find God's will for career endeavors? First, you walk with integrity in all your dealings at work and you walk with a generous heart. You offer grace and understanding to your coworkers and colleagues, knowing that human beings make mistakes and we're all in need of God's grace. When you walk out your faith each day at work in a godly fashion, you'll find that God will arrive before you do and show you the next step you're to take. Hard work and honesty are always in demand, regardless of the economy. Being the kind of employee that employers dream of puts usable material in the Lord's hands. He is the best agent a faithful job hunter can hope for.

How do you find someone to marry or improve your existing marriage? You walk with purity, as the Bible teaches. You become the kind of person you want to be married to. Are you looking for someone kind? Then grow in kindness. Are you looking for someone responsible? Then pay your bills on time. If you are looking for your spouse to be a person of prayer, then hit your knees. Become the person you want to be married to. Godliness is not a luxury or a bonus in dating or marriage (see 2 Cor. 6:14); it's a requirement. If you are a Christian and intend to obey God and marry a Christian, you need to be dating a Christ-follower. If you are married and desire greater godliness in your spouse, step it up yourself. So by doing God's will, you take a step further in finding His will. A German proverb sums it up: "Begin to weave, and God will give you the thread."

Too many times we stand dead still at a fork in the road, refusing to move and pleading for God to show us the way.

But He is saying, "If you will just walk with me, I will show you." The best way to *find* the will of God is to *do* the will of God. Mark Twain is alleged to have once said, "It ain't those parts of the Bible that I can't understand that bother me; it is the parts that I do understand." We already know much in our core about what is right and what is wrong. By living what we know, God is preparing us to live what we don't yet know. You can't do multiplication until you learn addition.

We prepare for the future by doing the next right thing. As Tommy Nelson says, "God hits moving targets." Doing God's will leads to discovering God's will. Each step on the mountainside of faith is a step closer to your burning bush. Even if you have someone else's sheep in tow on the far side of town, God may have a life-changing intersection for you around the next bend.

With God, the Ordinary Becomes Significant

What about that ordinary place where God spoke to Moses? It would have great significance later on. Ordinary places can become significant places very quickly. In a negative sense, the ordinary Texas School Book Depository became a significant place on November 22, 1963, when, through one of its windows, Lee Harvey Oswald fired the shot that killed President John F. Kennedy. And who had heard of Shanksville, Pennsylvania, before flight 93 crashed there on September 11, 2001? More positively, a rock in Plymouth Bay, Massachusetts, became the birthplace of the United States of America when William Bradford and the

Mayflower landed there. The significance of a place is determined by what happened there, in spite of a sign I once saw in a restaurant that read: "In 1862, absolutely nothing significant happened here."

To the contrary, the mount Moses was climbing would become one of the most significant places in Israel's history because of what happened there. In Exodus 3:12, God said to Moses, "When you have brought the people out of Egypt, you will worship God on this mountain." Later, in Deuteronomy 5:2, Moses said to the Israelites, "The LORD our God made a covenant with us at Horeb." Based on these two passages, some scholars believe that Horeb and Sinai, where Moses received the Law from God, might be different names for the same mountain, or perhaps Horeb and Sinai are peaks in the same mountain range. So the ordinary place where Moses was going about his ordinary work was really the epicenter of the will of God! This backside place of grazing for sheep was to be a place for God to speak, and His people to worship. Nothing could be more significant—and isn't that what we're longing for? "God, if You will speak clearly, I will worship deeply."

You never know where God might speak to you or what you might encounter in the course of an ordinary day. You may be faithfully following Him and come upon a situation that will change your life forever. God could speak to you in a conference room, a classroom, or a crowded stadium. The gathering you decide to attend just because you said you were hungry could become the very place you meet your future husband or wife. The employee you hire using your best judgment and insight could become the key to the future of your business. You never know. Neither did Moses. He shepherded the flock alone in a place he'd been before. But one day he showed up for work and God spoke. A bush burned. A voice called him by name. Suddenly nothing was the same. He was almost literally sitting on the very will of God, and until he saw the bush and heard the voice, he did not know it.

Some time ago, I undertook a house search for one of our family's remote controls. (We have four: a TV remote, a cable remote, a DVD remote and a stereo remote.) We had been missing the stereo remote for months, which meant I had to get up off the couch, walk over to the stereo to turn it on and adjust it, then walk all the way back to the couch to listen to it. One of the places I searched for the remote was the living room sofa. I removed all the cushions, and lo and behold, there it was. I had been sitting on the very thing I was looking for all along! Apparently, I'd been sitting on a few other items too: two pens, a stray Nerf dart from a game of father/son Nerf "warfare," and a photo of me next to a Corvette, taken at a local auto show. (I didn't get the car . . . just the picture.) I was a little disappointed that I didn't find any loose change; I thought the couch would be good for a couple bucks worth, for sure.

Moses on the backside of the mountain was perched right on top of God's will, although it took a burning bush to focus his attention on it. I believe that if we would simply walk with God in our ordinary routines, we would discover that He is present and waiting to show us His will. We might even find that we're sitting on the very thing we seek! The best way to find God's will is to do God's will. We are all sitting on top of the next right thing to do. By stepping instead of sitting, we can begin the process of discovery.

So pay attention right where you are. The answer you're seeking may be nearer than you think. The distance between standing up and kneeling down is only 15 or so inches. For Moses, an unremarkable job in a forgettable location, tending his father-in-law's lambs, turned out to be the recipe for living. Moses' willingness to do what he already knew to do primed the pump for God to speak. Our willingness in the ordinary things we know can do the same.

God's Will Is About God, Not Us

Most importantly, we must plant a stake of truth deeply in the ground that this thing called life is about Him . . . not us. Discovering our burning bush is not a spiritualization of our own plans. Too often we "baptize" our will and call it God's. He is not fooled, as He sees and knows the thoughts and intentions of the heart: "Nothing in all creation is hidden from God's sight. Everything is uncovered and laid bare before the eyes of him to whom we must give account" (Heb. 4:13).

When we're seeking God's will, our search can be more self-focused than God focused. We're asking ourselves, *What do I need to know?* Or, *Where should I be?* We're wondering, *What should I be doing?* instead of *What can I discover about God and His agenda?* Our prayer life becomes more asking God to bless our plans than to show us His.

Setting our hearts on His plan and His purpose is the key. God will not be fooled into mistaking our will for His own, or tricked into blessing us in whatever way we desire while we disregard Him. This may sound as if I am sending you to the

50-percent-off rack—inferring that God's will is less desirable than ours. The truth is, His will is the highest quality stuff—not the deeply discounted leftovers. His desire is far greater than ours. His plans supersede our plans; God's ways are infinitely higher than our own (see Isa. 55:8-9). As we cling to our mediocre desires based on someone else's life, He creates an original masterpiece just for us. The clinging brings fear; the release brings freedom.

For a long time, I was afraid of what God wanted to do in my life. You know, those "What if I'm sent to Africa?" type fears. Frankly, if God calls you to Africa, you'll be slumming anywhere else. David Livingstone, the famed British missionary to the "oh no, not there" continent of Africa, once stated, "I would rather be in the heart of Africa in the will of God than on the throne of England outside the will of God."[2] He understood that the heartbeat of the Father was also the place of his own greatest satisfaction.

The truth that God's will is about Him and not about us is a comfort, not a complication. The point at which we lay aside our fears marks the beginning of faith. I'm personally seeking to live in trust, not in fear, of God's will. We reach a new level of spiritual maturity when we can honestly say, "I am not afraid of God's will." Maybe you are not there yet. That's okay. Keep reading. Remember that our friend Moses is still wandering at this point; the bush has yet to speak! We are laying a foundation; the "Who" precedes the "what." God's will involves our career, our family, even our enjoyment of life; but first, it involves following God and fulfilling *His* agenda.

Clearly Tuned In

In September 1862, after the Union army lost the second Battle of Bull Run, President Abraham Lincoln wrote these words of reflection on the will of God:

> The will of God prevails. In great contests each party claims to act in accordance with the will of God. Both may be, and one must be wrong. God cannot be for and against the same thing at the same time. In the present Civil War it is quite possible that God's purpose is something different from the purpose of either party.[3]

President Lincoln understood that in spite of his desire that the Union army prevail and the war be quickly ended, God might have a different plan in mind. His purposes are not always crystal clear to us, but His heart to be known by His children never wavers. Ever. Revealing Himself is His desire, and once discovering Him becomes *our* desire, the world tilts in a different direction and our pursuits begin to accommodate His purpose. If we embrace that shift, we will be well on our way to knowing Him and knowing His plan for our lives.

My in-laws live in a tiny Texas town called Comfort. Seriously, that's the name of the place, and yes, it is comfortable. Plenty of wide-open space yawns between the ranch and our home in Houston. Driving back home from Comfort after a weekend there, Kelly and I tried to tune in the radio broadcast from our church. I had taken a Sunday off and wanted to check on things . . . I mean, hear a word from the Lord. We must have been at a point in the road where the signal was weak, because for a few moments we heard the guest speaker's message, and then it faded and we heard Brooks and Dunn singing "Boot Scoot Boogie." The mix of sermon and song sounded something like this: "Jesus is the . . . jump down, turn around, boot scootin', boogie . . . Heel, toe, doe-si-doe, Christ is at work in your heart . . . Trust Him boogie." Talk about mixed signals! One minute I was singing along, and the next minute I was praying. Mixed signals bring mixed messages. Bad reception results in bad theology.

Our lives are a little like that. We float back and forth from the holy to the mundane, from the profane to the silly and from the eternal to the temporal—but we need a fixed point, a strong signal by which to tune our hearts. Our own whims and wants and wishes are imperfect and fleeting, but His desires for us are steady and true. They are the fixed point by which we can recognize and understand everything else. Jesus said, "Seek first his kingdom and his righteousness, and all these things will be given to you as well" (Matt. 6:33). When we make Him our aim, He makes His aim clear. His signal never wavers; it plays clearly on the airwaves of our heart.

That day at the career fair, hundreds of my peers—my college classmates—found God's will for them. Without question, God calls people to the business community just as He does the mission field. Many connected with one of the opportunities presented, and the logo from one of the take-home trinkets soon began appearing on their paychecks. But not for me. The longer I wandered between the tables, the more confident I became of where I was supposed to go. I studied business and got the degree, but God created me for something else. My path was not being pitched by anyone there. Although I respect and honor those who took that route, it was not my route. My heart was beginning to see and recognize the flames of my own burning bush, and that afternoon was the one that confirmed for me my path in ministry. I walked out of the business building that day jobless but deeply confident. The bush continued to burn as I wandered a little farther around the backside of the mountain.

For Further Reflection and Discussion

1. Why do you want to know God's will?
2. Have you ever found yourself "on the backside of a mountain, tending someone else's sheep"? Describe that place.
3. What does this statement mean to you: "The best way to find the will of God is to do the will of God"? How can you apply that statement in your life?
4. Do you fear God's will, or welcome it? Why?
5. How comfortable are you with the assertion that the purpose and focus of your life should be about God, not about you?

Notes
1. M. Easton, *Easton's Bible Dictionary* (Oak Harbor, WA: Logos Research Systems, Inc., 1996), note on Exodus 2:10.
2. David Livingstone, cited in Ken Boa, "Discerning the Will of God," KenBoa.org. http://www.kenboa.org/text_resources/free_articles/5335.
3. Abraham Lincoln, "Meditation on the Divine Will," Washington, DC, September 1862. Cited in Roy B. Basler, *Collected Works of Abraham Lincoln* (Chapel Hill, NC: Rutgers University Press, 1953). http://showcase.netins.net/web/creative/lincoln/speeches/meditat.htm.

2

SHRUBBERY ABLAZE

Former New York Yankee second baseman Bobby Richardson once offered this brief and poignant prayer at a meeting of the Fellowship of Christian Athletes: "Dear God, Your will. Nothing more, nothing less. Amen." The power of such a sentence, if truly meant, is vast.

Richardson was no doubt sincere, and his prayer an admirable one. We, too, want nothing more and nothing less than His will for our lives, but by what process do we discover it? "How?" is a mission-critical question, and to answer it correctly, our mindset must be established before our mission is understood. In other words, the head must lead both the feet and the heart. The foundation of knowing God's will is to believe and trust in this truth: God's power always accompanies God's will.

We long to know God's will because we instinctively understand that a connection exists between God's will and His power. We sense that if we can determine what God wants us to do and then follow His leading, He will supply the strength, faith and joy we need in every circumstance. That hunch is correct. If we are walking in God's will, we will experience God's power. The two always go hand in hand. That's not to say we won't ever become tired or discouraged; but with the knowledge of His will, we can confidently say, "God, You called me into this, so I know You are with me here—and by Your power You're going to get me through it." God's will always has God's power. The two can't be separated. They go together like a hand in a glove, like peanut butter and jelly.

The fact that God's power accompanies His will removes the fear of hearing from Him and makes obedience to His will an opportunity for trusting, not for trying. If you have trusted Christ as your Savior, then the Holy Spirit lives inside of you. He is the very power of God in you. Your job is to place your trust in that power. This is a much different process than trying to figure out His plan on your own, then implement it through your own strength and wait until heaven to see if God is pleased.

Instead, we trust, we listen and we release control so that God might work through us. Look at the following verses, paying close attention to the emphasis noted:

I will give you a new heart and put a new spirit within you; I will remove from you your heart of stone and give you a heart of flesh. And *I will put my Spirit in you and move you to follow* my decrees and be careful to keep my laws (Ezek. 36:26-27).

We proclaim him, admonishing and teaching everyone to all wisdom, so that we may present everyone perfect in Christ. To this end I labor, struggling with all *his energy, which so powerfully works in me* (Col. 1:28-29).

So I find this law at work: When I want to do good, evil is right there with me. *For in my inner being I delight in God's law* (Rom. 7:21-22, emphasis added).

God's will—nothing more and nothing less—is based in His power—nothing more and nothing less. The discovery of the power source paves the way for the actual calling or task to be laid before us. If we receive His direction before we know His power, we set ourselves up for confusion at best, failure at worst.

Houston is "home" to NASA—and so, space exploration chatter is common in our city. The vast complex is located just a few miles south of town and is the destination of many a school field trip and tourist trek. I went there for the first time as an elementary school student, and 30 years later I took my son Greyson on his sixth birthday. The space program amazes me. If they ever need a chaplain for the space station, I'm signing up. I have a number of friends who work there, and one kindly submitted my name to sit in the Mission Control viewing gallery for a shuttle launch.

We were terribly excited as we pulled through the security checkpoints parking near the doors to Mission Control. As I walked in, I imagined background music playing and saw myself walking in slow motion to the door. (I didn't tell Kelly of my daydream; if I had, she would have said, "Houston, we have a problem. A BIG problem.") We were fortunate enough to sit in the gallery with 10 or so other people, and an astronaut slated for a subsequent mission handed us a flight manual as we listened to preflight communications between Mission Control and the flight crew. We were enthralled watching it all unfold.

Soon the checklists were complete, the engines ignited and the shuttle lifted off. Enormous tanks filled with fuel fired, and white smoke billowed from the launch pad. Not one person on that shuttle, in Mission Control or in our small gallery believed that the crew was powering the rocket. The launch was achieved on the strength of the rocket's engines, not the crew's power. They understood the power source prelaunch. They trusted in it to make their mission possible. The astronauts were to harness the power in order to allow it to lead them to the correct orbit. So it is with us. God's power is what propels the mission He's called us to. Regardless of where we're headed, the power is not ours to provide; it's His. The Spirit of God propels us.

Just Pay Attention

Moses' example gives us insight into this power. When he wandered onto the burning bush on the backside of Horeb, he did several things that led to further revelation from God. First, and very simply, he paid attention. You mean paying attention is an action item? It is. We live with thousands of distractions in the course of every day. Unfortunately, the meaningful things and the voice of the Lord can get lost in the overwhelming assault of distractions. Today's pace tempts us to handle the urgent and not the meaningful. Ralph Waldo Emerson said that "if the stars should appear but one night every thousand years, how man would marvel and stare."[1] But familiarity causes our attentiveness to drift. Not Moses. He was attentive to his surroundings and mindful that the bush he saw burning was very likely something more than a natural phenomenon. It wasn't just a smoldering campfire from some other shepherd's sojourn. It required a second look.

Many explanations have been suggested over the years for Moses' sighting of this fiery bush. Some have attributed its flames to St. Elmo's fire—a discharge of electricity that causes a kind of atmospheric glow. Others imagine that it could have been a volcanic phenomenon, or the firebrands of light that occur in dry lands with an abundance of storms, or even the brilliant (but not burning) blossoms of mistletoe twigs. Still others "explain away" the burning bush Moses saw by saying it was simply a myth, a psychological hallucination or a bright beam of sunlight reflected by the mountains. I once watched a television documentary trying to explain away the miracle of the burning bush. The scientific ideas presented were so extreme they required more faith than any Jew or Christian must exercise to believe in the divinely miraculous!

Call me unscientific, but here's my theory: I believe it was a real bush that really burned—and that Moses was aware enough of his surroundings and the Spirit of God to recognize it for what it was. Often it takes more faith to *not* believe than to believe. Attempts to explain away the miraculous are really just an attempt to dismiss the Creator or diminish His power and involvement in our lives. If we can reduce the miracle to natural phenomenon, we're the ones in charge. But if we sit back in awe and the rockets begin to rumble as Mission Control counts down "10, 9, 8, 7 . . ."—that's a totally different ride. Moses was aware enough of his surroundings and the Spirit of God to see the bush differently. He saw the miraculous in the mundane.

Since we're talking science, let's conduct a little experiment of our own: What do you think would happen if you picked a particular color today—say green—and decided to pay attention by looking for that color throughout the day? Don't you imagine you would notice several things that just "happened" to be that color? From grass and trees and street signs and traffic lights, life would become a paint-by-number palette with color #1 being green. Try it in the room you are reading in or when you are driving; look around and watch your attention to the color green light up the things you missed before. In the same way, imagine how life might change if you decided to take notice of the presence of God.

How mindful are you of spiritual things? Are you on the lookout for the hand of the Lord in your life? Too often we remain oblivious to the things God places in our path. We can't be bothered with burning bushes. We're too busy keeping an eye out for life's next latte, text message or errand to run. With our eyes focused on the prize of comfort or efficiency, we totally miss the higher things of the Kingdom. We drift.

> For the sun rises with scorching heat and withers the plant; its blossom falls and its beauty is destroyed. In the same way, the rich man *will fade away* even while he goes about his business (Jas. 1:11, emphasis added).

> Still others, like seed sown among thorns, hear the word; but the *worries of life*, the deceitfulness of wealth and the desires for other things come in *and choke the word*, making it unfruitful (Mark 4:18-19, emphasis added).

But not Moses. He noticed the bush. His gaze was set, nothing more and nothing less. Curious enough to temporarily abandon his shepherding agenda, he decided to investigate it. He came closer to see what there was to see.

Take Time to Investigate

Moses saw the burning bush. He noticed. He came closer to see why the bush was covered in flames but did not burn up. Miracles have a special way of demanding our attention. A bush on fire—who cares? But a burning bush that doesn't burn up? Whoa. That's something. A man on a cross? Thousands of criminals faced the same sentence by the Romans—but a crucified man whose sealed tomb is empty? Hang on now. Wisdom says to stop and investigate. Take it in.

We can go wrong in two ways during this part of the investigation process. We can either try to ignite our own burning bush, or we can attempt to douse the flame of God's. Neither approach is wise. Some of us are guilty of an "aim and flame" kind of faith: "Lord, look at the bush I just lit. Now keep it burning, will You?" You might have some great ideas—I'm sure you do—but God's will is better than your best idea, or mine. For a long time I was the managing partner of a little firm called God and Me, LLP. I lit the bush and expected Him to keep it going. But the truth is, my plans are limited in both vision and "kindling," so they tend to fizzle out. Many people grow cold toward God because He has not kept the bushes of their creation burning. But He is under no obligation to do so. Remember, this thing called life is about God, not about us. Don't believe that His job is just to bless our ideas. The bushes are His to light, not ours.

My ministry was completely revolutionized when I realized that sermon preparation was not simply a process of paying my dues with study and then asking Him to bless the message I prepared. My prayers for blessing and power were too late. I had already created the whole thing, with the right heart but in the wrong order. I was trying hard, too hard. The switch came when I became conscious that I had been asking Him to bless my ideas instead of asking Him for His idea. *God's power always accompanies God's will.*

As the light went on, I began to ask, "Lord, what do You want me to talk about? Lord, what is *Your* idea?" I was now seeking His will from the beginning instead of asking Him to bless my idea at the end. Again, my heart wasn't sinful—just uninformed. So, as He revealed my attempts at lighting the bush, I laid down the "aim and flame" lighter and kept my eye open for His match to strike.

It is true that we may be the arsonist of our own desires, but on the flip side, we can also become the firefighters of His. Because the vast majority of us are afraid of really hearing from the Lord, we scurry around trying to put out the flames He is kindling instead of fanning them. What if His burning bush is a check larger than I planned to write, a place I am afraid to go or a move that's not a part of my 5- or 10-year plan? What if it hurts? What if mission and ministry aren't just for someone else? So we try to extinguish the bush God has lit.

Now would be a good time to settle this in your heart: Whatever you have planned isn't likely to happen anyway, and life sometimes *does* hurt—but God's will is always preferable to any design of our own we could concoct. He is not asking us to either set bushes on fire *or* smother them. He's asking us to draw closer and be inquisitive and open to the possibility that *He is behind the fire.*

God Bushes Keep Burning

It's curious to me that the bush never burned up. You know, your ideas and plans and mine will burn up and die out at some point, but God's do not. They never will. I assume that you have a laundry list of ideas and dreams for yourself or your family that are wonderful. The proof of the power behind them is their ability to last. Your strength isn't enough. We can work hard, but we can't keep bushes burning. Trust that *God's power always accompanies His will* and put the lighter fluid down. The freedom of faith will allow you to follow that job lead and keep interviewing until the fire dies out. If it doesn't, that may be the job for you. Accept that invitation to a date and see where it goes. If it dies out, fine. If it doesn't, keep following in faith. (And by the way, singles, the only thing you need to decide on date number one is whether or not there will be a date number two!) If the fire continues to burn, it just might lead to a marriage made in heaven. Your assignment and mine is not to predict the outcome, but to simply draw close and observe. Take the risk to investigate.

Allow God to put a match to the bush or snuff out the fire as He desires. To set a course of our own design is detrimental. A fun run in Cleveland once considerably decreased in "fun" when the driver of the pace car took a wrong turn, leading 200 to 300 runners some three miles out of the way.[2] Some of the runners must have been thinking, *Man, this is one tough race. I thought I was farther along.* They were prepared for six miles but ended up with nine. We can do the same thing following our own plan and running in our own strength.

Trust me. You don't want the responsibility of keeping life ignited by your own efforts. You will waste your strength running the wrong course. A listening ear beats swift feet every time.

For Further Reflection and Discussion

1. Why is the truth that "God's power always accompanies God's will" important to understand?
2. What "strange sight" turned out to be God's leading in your life?
3. When have you tried to light your burning bush or extinguish His?
4. Why do His fires never burn out?
5. Describe a time when you ran a longer race because you weren't following God?

Notes

1. Ralph Waldo Emerson, "Nature," 1836. www.vcu.edu/engweb/transcendentalism/au thors/emerson/essays/naturetext.html.
2. Jean Dubail, The Plain Dealer, "Rite Aid Cleveland 10K Takes a Wrong Turn," Cleave land.com, May 20, 2007. http://blog.cleveland.com/sports/2007/05/wrong_turn_turns_ rite_aid_clev.html.

3

A Barefoot Man's Surrender

When Moses came closer to the burning bush, an angel of the Lord spoke to him from within the bush: "Moses, Moses!" and Moses responded, "Here I am." This was no ordinary encounter. It was a special, personal appearance of God to an aging exile working as a shepherd—and the purpose of the "visit" was to lead this shepherd into a new "shepherding" role. God had chosen Moses to lead His people out of Egypt and into the land He promised to them hundreds of years before. By drawing closer to the bush, Moses was drawing closer to the will of God. His attentiveness was yielding fruit. Wandering was becoming listening, and listening would become purpose.

This kind of deliberate, thoughtful inquiry goes against almost everything in our culture. Our church's missions pastor, William Taylor, often reminds his Type A, get-'er-done pastor (that would be me), "We need to give time for God to move." Patient inquiry takes us a step closer to a wise and reasoned decision. Focused attention draws us close and enables us to see the miraculous.

My call to vocational ministry was this kind of "drawing near" process. I grew up in a single-parent home. I was not in church every week and did not become a Christian until I was a high school junior. If you had asked every person in my class to name the student most likely to become a pastor, I doubt that a single one would have voted for me. Like a chameleon changing colors to fit in to his environment, the strength of my character changed to match the peers that surrounded me. I experimented with alcohol, and even once with marijuana. My memories of that time make me grateful to have survived some of the escapades I was involved in, and remind me of the long way God has faithfully brought me. Those were days of immaturity more than rebellion, but nonetheless not ones to model to my children. I was a decent kid underneath the "cool"—but I was lost. Wandering.

As a high school graduate, I went on a summer missions trip to Montana with our student ministry. I was headed to Texas A&M University in just a couple of months, but God wanted to plant a seed of calling in my life. There in Gardner, Montana, in a church that seated about 50, I wrestled with God's calling for the first of many times. I heard Him saying He wanted me in vocational ministry. I simply said no. (Actually, it may have been something more like "Are you *kidding* me?") Back and forth we went until I could finally pray, as Jesus did, "Lord, not my will but Yours be done." When I did, I was comforted with a sense of peace, and the bush He lit began to burn with an even brighter flame. It wasn't until years later that I fully understood this spark. But this moment of "Yes, Lord" in Montana was the beginning step of finding God's will for my vocational life. Years later, I brought my wife and son to visit the little church where this all took place. What a teachable moment to say to my son, "Right there is where Daddy first heard God calling him to ministry." It built my faith to look back, and it planted a seed in his heart to hear from God.

When Moses moved toward the bush, *then* God spoke. Do you see it? "When *the LORD saw that he had gone over to look,* God called to him from within the bush, 'Moses! Moses!'" (Exod. 3:4, emphasis added). Not until he went over to investigate this strange sight did God call him by name. Some of the "strange sights" in your life will be God. Some of them will just be strange sights, and nothing more. But when you walk toward the bush and begin to hear His voice, pay attention! In Moses' day, to speak a man's name twice in greeting was a sign of friendship and affection. God called Moses' name twice. His "Moses, Moses" said "I know you. I have a plan for you."

Moses' Mission

And Moses simply replied, "Here I am." Now, I can think of plenty that he could have said and didn't. He could have said, "Here I am. Finally, You get back around to me" or "Remember me? Moses, the guy who grew up rich in Pharaoh's house? The one who went to the temple of the sun and had all those clever teachers and showed such promise as a leader?" or maybe, "I'm glad you found me out here leading sheep after all these years. Yeah. Here I am. Moses. Nice to see *You* again, God. Where have You been?"

But he simply said, "Here I am." It probably took the patience and self-control learned from every one of his 40 years of shepherding in Midian to shorten his answer. The ability to answer with clarity and brevity requires years of maturity. The assertion of Moses' abilities had been sanded over time to a smooth submission.

I have a little ottoman in my study at home that I've spent a lot of time on . . . face down. I just press my face into that footrest and pray, "Lord, here I am." Not, here I am with pastoral preparation. Not, here I am with experience as a speaker. Not, here I am with my entire congregation, or with my family, or with higher education. Just "Here I am." I'm convinced that God is not too terribly interested in our résumé. He's glad for it—sure. He filled it in! But He's not asking us to show it to Him to validate who we are. He's just asking us to say, "Here I am," and then listen to what He's got to say. It took Moses 40 years to say those words. Please don't wait that long or require a road that tough! Waiting before the Lord tunes our ears to His voice and welcomes His presence. This isn't just a quick "Here I am" while rushing to the next thing. Moses' "Here I am" said "I am willing to cast aside all else now to hear from heaven."

Being called by name to journey to your destined aim is like sweet salve to the soul. Someone has said that the two most comforting words any person can hear are their own name and the word "home." A personal call to a safe place puts our heart at ease. It erases fear. When God said "Moses, Moses!" it was a personal call from the Creator to Moses, with the aim of bringing His people home. God calls you by name too. He knows every thought in your mind, every secret thing about you. And you can be sure that the plans He has for you are custom made, exactly suited to you and perfectly timed for His purpose. He is able to bring together our varied experiences, our spiritual gift-edness and His purposes. God knows you better than any personality test, and He will use His complete knowledge of you for your good and His glory.

I graduated high school with low test scores and only two extracurricular activities to my name. I realized my junior year that the yearbook published senior credits chronicling each student's achievements and activities, and I feared that all I would have after my name would be a semicolon separating me from the next person: "Gregg Matte; Michele McMahon . . ." So I joined Students for Christ and Health Occupations Students of America. (I had planned to be an orthodontist ever since I saw my mom write a check to mine. Truly.)

With my low SAT scores, my woefully short list of extracurricular activities and a "top 50%" class ranking, major colleges weren't biting. But God had a call for me that fit. I was (miraculously, I believe) accepted at Texas A&M University, and I remember praying in that small church in Montana, "Lord, let A&M be known as a Christian university by the time I leave." Pretty bold for a kid who didn't exactly set Alief Elsik High School on fire. But I knew something: I was a weak man with a strong God. I was going to this big state college for a degree, but He knew I was going for His purpose. I ultimately graduated with a marketing degree, which has been helpful in ministry, but I didn't leave A&M for 10 years after I graduated.

A home Bible study that my roommates and I began, called "Breakaway," exploded into a fire God caused to burn, and believe me—it was a strange sight. I drew near and listened. What started as several students in my living room eventually became thousands of students meeting in Reed Arena (the university's basketball venue) each week for worship and teaching. Worship leaders like Chris Tomlin, Shane and Shane, Ross King, Michael Armstrong, Stephen Smith and others cut their teeth with us. The ministry is still going strong today under the leadership of Ben Stuart. This year they met at Kyle Field (A&M's football stadium) with over 7,500 students present.

It turned out that Aggieland was the perfect fit for me, although I wasn't its perfect student. It wasn't about the traditions, sports or scholarship for me, but about God using me, shaping me and preparing me for what I'm doing now as pastor of Houston's First Baptist Church. Believe me when I say that I was (and am) an unlikely candidate for either assignment. But I'm grateful that God said "Gregg, Gregg!" as I walked closer to the flame. I'm glad I was caught up in His fire, instead of asking Him to squirt lighter fluid on my small plans to make money by straightening teeth. (For the record, though, I think orthodontists are great—and I think of mine with gratitude every time I smile.) Realizing that I was a weak man with a strong God changed everything.

Here-I-Am Surrender

Sara Groves is one of my favorite singers. I don't know her personally, but her music has truly impacted me, particularly her song called "Remember Surrender." Sara's lyric echoes Moses' words, "Here I am": "Remember surrender, remember the rest, remember that weight lifting off of your chest, *and realizing it's not up to you and it never was.*"[1] It wasn't up to Moses to fulfill

God's plan. It was up to God. Moses simply saw a strange sight, drew closer and heard a voice. All that was required of him was surrender.

Don't get me wrong; goal-setting is good. But surrendering to the Divine is divine. Discovering God's will for your life does not result from deal making with the Almighty, but begins instead with surrender. Don't plan the next 10 years of your career on one good interview, or name your future children on the third date. God has a trajectory in mind for you that is right and good and not at all dependent on the perceived strengths of your long-range planning skills. Watchman Nee puts it like this: "To have God do His own work through us, even once, is better than a lifetime of human striving."[2]

Surrender in war is an admission of defeat; surrender in life is the seed of victory. It is a lifelong process of releasing control and grasping trust. It might seem that this kind of "giving up" to the divine plan of God would get easier with age—shouldn't Moses have had it down at 80?—but that's not the case. It actually gets more difficult the older we become. I remember being able to fit everything I owned into my Honda Prelude, and now it would take two semitrucks and a realtor to move me up the street a block. Stability surrounded by stuff is the cul-de-sac on which most of us live. Like the late Rich Mullins sang, "Surrender don't come natural to me; I'd rather fight You for something I don't really want than take what You give that I need."[3] Don't let your heart get in a rut. Continue to surrender to the call of God by saying "Here I am" when you hear His voice, just as Moses did.

The Bible is filled with "Here I am" responses, with large and small surrenders to God's beckoning voice. Isaiah said, "Here am

I. Send me!" (Isa. 6:8). Peter accepted Jesus' invitation to leave the safety of his boat for a nighttime stroll on the waves (see Matt. 14:28-32). Jesus Himself answered God's call to the cross with the words, "May your will be done" (Matt. 26:42). Is there any other way but surrender? Well, yes and no. We can refuse to listen, and refuse to surrender, but we do so at our own peril. Surrendering our agenda to God's makes sense, because His way is best. Always.

As I was working on this chapter, I had the opportunity to put my words into practice. I had gone to our church's retreat center out in the country for a day of focused writing. Not much happens out there—except maybe a car an hour that passes on the Farm-to-Market road that fronts the property. But the day I was crafting this section on surrender, I looked up from my work to see a man peering through the window at me! Now, I'm a city guy, so to me, a stranger on the porch means it's probably time to call the police. I asked him what he needed in a "go away" tone of voice, and he said, "a phone."

Good, I thought. *I'm off the hook. This house doesn't have a phone. Surely my cell phone doesn't count, right, God? And I don't have a lot of time for a dangerous looking country boy whose tractor is out of gas. I'm working on Your book.* But seeing no way out, I met him at the door and let him use my cell to call the owner of the pasture he was mowing to request more diesel. (This is Texas, after all, so this kind of story checks out.)

As he waited, we began to chat; and as we did, I realized this was a "Here I am" moment of surrender for me. My plan was good, but God's was bound to be better. So I surrendered the book for a few minutes and focused on my new friend Daniel, a guy in his late thirties who found it very interesting that I was writing about knowing God's will. Wouldn't you know it, he asked me how to go about finding God's will in the area of love. I just happened to have a few notes ready and gave him the short version of this chapter verbally. Then he took off his dusty cowboy hat and bowed his head, and we prayed together.

If I hadn't walked toward the strange sight at my window and surrendered my agenda for a few moments, I would have missed a great opportunity to connect and be used by God to meet a need. God knew Daniel's tractor would run out of gas at about the same time I was writing a section about surrender. In his divine plan, the two of us got to worship God together at the intersection of hay and concrete. Not a bad day's work.

Barefoot Worship

As we participate in the process of knowing God's will by paying attention to those "burning bushes" of our lives, stepping closer and investigating, listening and coming to a place of surrender, we are inevitably led to worship. Moses was too:

> When the LORD saw that he had gone over to look, God called to him from within the bush, "Moses, Moses!" And Moses said, "Here I am." "Do not come any closer," God said. "Take off your sandals, for the place where you are standing is holy ground" (Exod. 3:4-5).

God's presence in the burning bush was something known as a theophany, or an appearance or manifestation of God in a temporary form perceptible to the human senses. In other words, God's appearing to man in a way that man could see and discern. Moses saw God, but he saw Him in representative form, as an angel of the Lord. The angel of the Lord was a true and real manifestation of God, but not the fullness of Him.

Moses' response to this theophany, this appearance of God, was the recognition that he stood in the presence of the Holy. The Lord said that His presence there on the mountain made the very ground on which Moses stood "holy ground." God called Moses by name and spoke to him directly. The weight of that personal meeting, and God's instruction to "Take off your shoes" drove Moses to respond in humility.

Louie Giglio says, "Worship is our response, both personal and corporate, to God for who He is and what He has done, expressed in and by the things we say and how we live."[4] Moses personally responded to God's holy presence by drawing near and, as a sign of reverence and respect, removing his shoes. Then, as Moses hid his face, God revealed to him what He planned to do through Moses on behalf of his people. He told Moses how He would defeat enemy nations (and He even called them by name!), rescue the Israelites and bring them out of Egypt and into the Promised Land (see Exod. 3:7-10). At God's direction, Moses humbly removed his shoes, an act that was seen as a sign of respect toward a superior, and an Eastern custom when entering another person's dwelling. Moses was acknowledging his humility before God, and his presence in the holy place of God.

The holy ground God referred to was not a place; the holy ground was God's presence. Moses had been in this place before, with no need to humble himself or remove his shoes. But this time, God was there—and His presence changed everything.

The presence of God makes ordinary places holy. Listen to that sentence again, thinking about your life. The presence of God makes ordinary places holy. Your cubicle or your kitchen is a holy place because of the presence of God. God does that in our hearts through the cross of Christ, and with our lives through our burning bushes. Our ordinary hearts and our everyday lives have the presence of the Holy.

Because he was on holy ground, God asked Moses to remove his shoes. Being barefoot is being vulnerable too. You're most likely to go barefoot in your own home. At home you will kick off your shoes and relax because you know you are safe and secure. You don't likely go to work barefoot, or hike or play basketball barefoot. But at home you forgo shoes because at home you can let down your guard. Did you know that the place of greatest security in the world is the center of God's will? It is not always worry-free, or trouble-free, but it is secure because it is where your holy Father calls you to serve.

Think about little babies' bare feet. They don't need socks or shoes on those tiny feet because you, their parent, are going to keep them safe. You are not going to let their feet be scraped on a rock or set down on hot pavement. Until they are able to walk, a baby's shoes are mostly for decoration, not for protection. Their soft, vulnerable feet are protected, even without cover.

In God's presence we are humble and ready to worship. In God's will we are vulnerable but securely "at home." Moses drew near to God, and made himself humble and vulnerable as he worshiped barefoot. He did not want to run from the burning bush or extinguish it. He wanted to move in closer to the presence of God and respond to His holiness. God's will is discovered in reverence and in seeking. In a vulnerable heart of worship we discover the God of "God's will."

Are you seeking God? Do you want to more deeply discover His will? The next time you see a burning bush—a sight or an opportunity that might be orchestrated by Him—pay attention. Draw near. Listen. Surrender. And respond to Him in worship. You might even want to slip off your shoes, reminding yourself that in His holy presence you are closer to home than you've ever been before, wanting His will. God's will, nothing more, nothing less.

For Further Reflection and Discussion

1. How well do you draw near to listen?
2. What needs to be surrendered before you can focus on God and remain attentive to His voice?
3. How have Rich Mullins' words, "I'd rather fight you for something I don't really want than take what You give that I need," been true in your life?
4. What was your primary takeaway from this chapter? Your primary application point?

Notes

1. Sara Groves, "Remember Surrender," from the album *All Right Here* (Mobile, AL: Integrity Media, Inc., 2003). Emphasis added.
2. Watchman Nee, *A Table in the Wilderness* (Fort Washington, PA: Christian Literature Crusade 2005).
3. Rich Mullins, "Hold Me Jesus," from the album *Songs* (Brentwood, TN: Reunion Records, Inc., 1995).
4. Louie Giglio, *The Air I Breathe* (Sisters, OR: Multnomah, 2003), p. 70.

4

IT'S ABOUT GOD: THE "WHO" PRECEDES THE "WHAT"

Years ago, when I was in college, a friend of mine and I went to Harlingen, Texas, and decided to cross over the border into Mexico. When we did, we saw a sign for $2 haircuts. Well, we were students and didn't have a lot of money—so a $2 haircut seemed too good a deal to pass up. Once we were inside the shop I thought I might as well try to practice my Spanish a little, so I tried to converse with the señorita who was cutting my hair. She looked to be only a year or two older than us, and was eager to "chat" with college guys.

As I was talking to this woman, I wanted to tell her that my friend and I would be leaving Mexico later that evening. So I said, "*Nosotros bailamos esta noche.*" (Some of you already are way ahead of me here and can see trouble coming.) She became very excited, because "*nosotros bailamos*" does not mean "we go," but "we dance."

"*Nosotros bailamos esta noche?*" she repeated. "*Si! Si! Nosotros bailamos!*" Translation, in our best James Bond voice, "Yes, tonight we dance."

My friend was shaking his head, listening to my *bailamos* instead of *vamos* and at the same time saying to his barber, "Not so short! Not so short!" My barber was not happy. She had been thinking two American boys were going to take her dancing after work, but instead they were leaving right after their haircuts!

"No, no, no," I corrected, backpedalling as fast as I could. "*Nosotros* vamos *esta noche. Nosotros vamos.*" But the deal had already gone bad. She did not get to go dancing, and I did not get a good haircut—not even for $2. Just two little words, *vamos* and *bailamos*, but boy, there was a world of difference between them. Just like there is a world of difference between "God's will" and "my life." If we get fixated on the wrong word, we're not likely to get where we're going, or like where we wind up!

You may be reading this book to answer the question "What is God's will for my life?" But we don't get far in the pursuit of God's will before we discover that we may be focusing on the wrong thing, or at least in the wrong order. Is your emphasis on "God's will" or "my life"? You see, before we can reliably know and understand God's will, we must know God Himself. Any discussion of God's will must begin with God. That's where we have gotten so confused. Instead of beginning the subject with Him, we begin it with us. Clarity comes when who He is becomes elevated over what we are to do. In the matter of finding God's will, the "who" of Him always precedes the "what" for us.

Moses saw a bush burning and drew closer to it. He heard a voice speak and listened to it. He heard a call and answered it. And he did not just discover God's will . . . he discovered the *God* of God's will. When someone comes to me seeking to know the will of God, they often say something like this: "Pastor, I really need to know God's will for my life in this area." Almost always, the emphasis is on the last part of the request: "my life." That little pronoun "my" may look small, but it plays big. Whether they realize it or not, the key focus in their request should be "God"—not "my."

Discovering God's will can become a selfish and self-centered game when the focus—spoken or unspoken—is not on God at all, but on us. That one small pronoun can steer us way off course in seeking God's will, in the same way that a few small degrees of navigation can send a plane or a ship far from its intended destination. The small things matter!

When Moses heard the voice of God speak from the burning bush, God didn't first speak His planned direction of Moses' life. Instead God spoke about Himself. As you read the following verses, underline all the times you see "I" and circle all the times you see "you."

> I am the God of your father, the God of Abraham, the God of Isaac, and the God of Jacob . . . I have surely seen the affliction of my people who are in Egypt and have heard their cry because of their taskmasters. I know their sufferings, and I have come down to deliver them out of the hand of the Egyptians and to bring them up out of that land to a good and broad land, a land flowing with milk and honey, to the place of the Canaanites, the Hittites, the Amorites, the Perizzites, the Hivites, and the Jebusites. And now, behold, the cry of the people of Israel has come to me, and I have also seen the

oppression with which the Egyptians oppress them. Come, I will send you to Pharaoh that you may bring my people, the children of Israel, out of Egypt (Exod. 3:6-10, *ESV*).

Do you see the use of pronouns in God's address to Moses? Six times God says "I have" or "I am" or "I will." He tells Moses who He is, what He has done and what He plans to do. *Then* God brings Moses into the conversation: "I will send *you* . . ." He tells Moses. God surely had a plan for Moses. But first He had things to teach Moses about Himself. There are six "I's" and two "yous" for a reason. The first thing we need to know about God's will is God Himself!

The grand "I" of Scripture is not us; therefore, we must understand the attributes of His character. We waste too much time trying to tell our Creator who we are and what we want. Instead, we should be discovering who He is and what He wants. From the burning bush to the Red Sea, Moses is discovering the attributes of God, and at this leg of the journey, he will learn that God is compassionate, caring, self-existent and trusted provider. Embracing each of these traits will encourage us to trust His will over our own.

Compassionate and Caring

God is compassionate and caring. We may incorrectly think of Him more as a cruel taskmaster, but in truth, He is compassionate and caring. We imagine that if we follow His will He is going to be a slave driver, demanding of us, "Go more. Do more.

Be more. Give more." But God sees and hears the cries of His people. He cares for them. At the time when God appears to Moses in the burning bush, the Israelites have been in slavery for 400 years. Four hundred years! That means a child was born into slavery, lived in slavery and died in slavery. And so did his child. And his grandchild. And his great-grandchild! None of them were rescued. None of them were set free. But God saw, heard and had compassion on His people.

If you imagine God as mercilessly demanding, then your picture of the Father is distorted and needs adjusting. He has great compassion on us. He has compassion on our lusts. Compassion on our addictions. Compassion on our secret thoughts. Compassion on our insecurities. He cares for us. Remarkably, He has compassion on us even with regard to those things He does not approve and did not cause! If we're honest, we would have to admit that many of the hurts in our lives come about when we decide to ignore God and go our own way. We hope God is not looking, or that He will at least blink and miss our premeditated choice to sin. We rebuff Him and stubbornly make our own way, then end up in a world of hurt. That's when God says, "I love you. I feel compassion toward you. And I'm coming after you."

Compassion has been called "a sympathetic consciousness of others' distress together with the desire to alleviate it."[1] God doesn't just glance our way and say, "Poor schmucks, I feel so sorry for them. I wish I could do something." No! He sees our struggles with sin and self and circumstances, and He says, "Oh, how I hurt, because My children hurt! I'm going to do something for them, even though they don't deserve it. And even if they do not ask."

His compassion on the children of Israel went far beyond feeling or emotion. As V. Raymond Edman states in *The Disciplines of Life*, "God's compassion . . . is demonstrated by definite acts to testify his covenant with Israel. God's compassion steps forward into the mess that you and I make of our lives and hugs and loves and rescues us. That's what God does."[2]

With the compassionate heart of a father, God offers His love in the midst of difficult times. And He asks us to do the same. Monday, August 29, 2005, spelled disaster for the great city of New Orleans, as Hurricane Katrina swept in. At the time, I didn't realize how severely our part of the Gulf Coast would be affected. Soon after the dreaded storm, buses and cars began to roll into Houston filled with the displaced citizens of New Orleans. The hotel down the street from our church brimmed with people, as did the stream of cars with Louisiana plates, filled with whatever possessions could be salvaged. The packed hotel opened a ministry door for us as we fed hundreds each night and gave away everything from diapers to deodorant. The two best things we did, oddly enough, were setting up computers in the fellowship hall for the out-of-town folks to send and receive email, and opening our gym for their kids to play and just be kids.

Prior to this hurricane, I had prayed for our church to grow in its cultural diversity. Little did I know that God was about to use the devastating storm as an answer to my prayer. Franklin Avenue Baptist Church, the largest African-American church in our denomination, was headed our way. Knowing the compassionate heart of God, we flung open our arms and our church doors to them. What a blessing they were and still are to us! Their spirit and diversity blessed us as much or more than our compassion blessed them. Because we know, love and serve a compassionate God, there was no hesitation or delay in helping our brothers and sisters. As Christians, we knew just how to help them see heaven in us.

One moment I'll never forget was when we delivered their American flag back to them in New Orleans. It had been submerged in the floodwaters and had been hanging as a sign of unity in our foyer since the storm. When I walked into Franklin Avenue's reopened worship center, carrying the flag, the place erupted in celebration. As Christians and Americans, the compassion of God crossed state and racial lines. That night we were just brothers and sisters celebrating our compassionate and caring God.

The God Without a Birth Certificate

"I am who I am," God told Moses, as Moses doubted himself and his abilities when he heard the assignment that God had in mind:

> He said, "But I will be with you, and this shall be the sign for you, that I have sent you: when you have brought the people out of Egypt, you shall serve God on this mountain." Then Moses said to God, "If I come to the people of Israel and say to them, 'The God of your fathers has sent me to you,' and they ask me 'What is his name?' what shall I say to them?" God said to Moses, "I AM WHO I AM." And he said, "Say this to the people of Israel, 'The LORD, the God of your fathers, the God of

Abraham, the God of Isaac, and the God of Jacob, has sent me to you.' This is my name forever, and thus I am to be remembered throughout all generations" (Exod. 3:12-15, *ESV*).

Who is this God, of whom we desire to know His will? He is the compassionate and caring One, but He is also I AM THAT I AM. What does that odd phrase mean? It means that God is both timeless and self-existent. Past, present and future, he is I AM THAT I AM. There was never a time past when God hoped to be something He was not; and there will never be a time future when He will wish He could have been something else. God is always exactly who He is. He is perfection. He has no past date of birth. He has no future date of death. He is, and has always been, the everpresent "dash" in between. No one created Him. No one can slay Him. He is timeless.

The writer of Hebrews wrote, "Jesus Christ is the same yesterday and today and forever" (Heb. 13:8). Jesus said, "Before Abraham was born, I am!" (John 8:58). The capitalized "LORD" in His speech to Moses is actually Y-H-W-H, a word so holy that it was not even spoken in Jewish culture. It is mentioned 6,000 times in the Old Testament and represents the covenant name of God. It means, "I am who I am."

This same YHWH is our present-tense covenant God. Do you need hope? Well, He doesn't just give hope; He *is* hope. Do you need strength? He doesn't just give strength; He Himself *is* strength. Do you need love? He doesn't just give love; He *is* love—present-tense, active love. The God of God's will is the "I am that I am." He's the Lord God Almighty—the God of

Abraham, Isaac, Jacob, and you! Beth Moore says it like this: "God is the God of your was, He is the God of your is, and He is the God of your is to come."[3]

God's Will Never Lacks God's Provision

The God of "God's will" is compassionate and caring, and He is timeless and self-existent. He is also the God who provides. This is a good thing, because we are needy people. No matter how much wealth we accrue, or how many accolades we receive, we remain needy. And God is good with that. In fact, He planned it that way. He created us with unquenchable thirst to draw us to the well of life: Himself! I must admit that it's difficult for this planning, self-confident, driven author to admit neediness. I find it hard to type these words on my Mac much less embrace them. But my God is a God who provides, and I am His needy child.

One of my heroes of the faith is George Müller, a German-born evangelist who preached, and founded orphanages, in England, in the 1800s. Müller was known as a man of prayer who believed God would provide, and he saw God do so over and over again. The story is told of a morning in the orphanage when there was no food to be found. Cups, plates and bowls were at the table and the children stood waiting for their meal, but the pantry was empty, and there was no money to buy food. Müller bowed his head and prayed, "Dear Father, we thank Thee for what Thou art going to give us to eat." Then there was a knock at the door. The neighborhood baker stood before Müller and said, "I could not sleep last night. Somehow I felt that you didn't have bread for breakfast, and the Lord wanted me to send you some. So I got up at 2:00 A.M. and baked some fresh bread, and have brought it." Müller thanked the man and had no sooner closed the door than the milkman, too, knocked on it. His milk cart had broken down right in front of the orphanage, and he wanted to give the children all the milk he carried so that he could empty his wagon and repair it![4] God's will never lacks God's provision. As God spoke to Moses in the burning bush, He revealed Himself and then revealed His intent to provide for His people:

> So I have come down to rescue them from the hand of the Egyptians and to bring them up and out of that land into a good and spacious land, a land flowing with milk and honey (Exod. 3:8).

And when He led His people out of bondage in Egypt, they did not go empty-handed:

> And I will make the Egyptians favorably disposed toward this people, so that when you leave you will not leave empty-handed. Every woman is to ask her neighbor and any woman living in her house for articles of silver and gold and for clothing, which you put on your sons and daughters. And so you will plunder the Egyptians (Exod. 3:21-22).

Do you realize when this "plundering" took place? It happened as the sun was rising the morning after the first Passover, when every firstborn of every Egyptian household lay dead.

Amazingly, the Israelites' requests were not met with anger or derision by the Egyptians, but with *favor*. Much is said today about the "favor" of God. But today's flavor of favor is often a thin spiritual veneer for fleshly greed. How can you tell the difference between a request made for personal gain and a request made for the glory of God? It's simple. What is the ultimate end of that request? Is it self-satisfaction or is it worship? The plundering of the Egyptians allowed the Israelites to leave their lives of slavery and freely worship God. That was Moses' request to Pharaoh: "This is what the LORD says: Let my people go *so that they may worship me*" (Exod. 8:20, emphasis added). They weren't just moving from downtown Egypt to a nicer place in the suburbs! They meant to worship their God on the journey no matter how far He led them. Moses called their exodus a "three day journey" to worship the LORD. That idiom meant "a major trip with formal consequences," and Pharaoh knew it.[5] He knew they were asking for leave to go and worship their God. By all means, their life was going to improve, but that was not the goal. Worshiping God is the only goal that keeps you in the game when the desert is hot and the food is scarce.

Even though they were slaves in Egypt, the Israelites would leave with great riches, because the God of God's will *provides*. We've already said that God's will is always accompanied by God's power. Here is another promise you can take to the bank: *God's will never lacks God's supply.* He promised to supply all that the Israelites would need for their journey, and He did. Hudson Taylor, missionary to China in the 1800s, put it like this: "God's work done in God's way will never lack God's supply."

How crazy was it that slaves asked their owners for their richest possessions and received them! Ladies, what do you suppose might happen if you went door to door in your neighborhood and asked for the best clothing and jewelry your neighbors possess? Can you see yourself standing on your neighbor's porch and saying, "Hi. I'm your neighbor from down the street, and I'm on a kind of scavenger hunt. I wonder if I might have all your precious jewelry (nothing costume, please!), your watch, your engagement and wedding rings, oh—and the nicest clothes in your closet too. I can promise you it's for a good cause."

Most likely you would be looking at a very agitated neighbor or perhaps even a door slammed in your face! But God provided for His people in just this way. The Bible uses the Hebrew word for "plunder." Do you know how you get plunder? After you have won a war. But the Israelites didn't do battle with the Egyptians to receive God's provision. He battled the Egyptians Himself with mighty miracles, and the victory was His. God fought the battle on the Israelites behalf, and they received the plunder. In a way, you could say that they received payment with interest in a single night for 400 years of slavery. God provided for them, and He will provide for you.

A provision of plunder can be seen in this true story of a friend of mine. Picture a music minister's home, with six kids, in a small Illinois town. If you have in your head the bare necessities combined with jovial, constant chaos, you are on the right track. The table at the Bolins' house always had food on it, but dining out and big vacations were nonexistent. They were also a family desperately in need of a break since Molly, their eight-year-old child with special needs, and her grandfather had recently died.

One day, a strong Midwestern wind had blown some trash into their yard the day it was to be mowed. Dad sent the kids out to pick up the trash before the mower string was pulled. As the trash was gathered, one of the seven picked up an empty cup from McDonald's. The debate still rages as to which kid actually found the cup, but it had an unrevealed game card on the side. Instead of throwing the cup into the trash bag, they pulled the tab to see the words "Free Trip to Disney World for the entire family." The minister's family, who had never ordered dessert at a restaurant, was on its way to Disney! To sweeten the deal, food was included and the waiters' tips were paid for based upon the amount of food served. So every meal for the six kids and parents was endless. A vacation of a lifetime, filled with theme parks and food, provided by a cup that "happened" to blow into their yard on the right day. Sounds like the God who provides to me!

Not only did God provide silver and gold for Moses' people, but He also provided a destination for them that would prove more satisfying than Orlando was for the Bolinses. He told Moses that a "good and spacious land" was before them, "a land flowing with milk and honey" (Exod. 3:8). What in the world does that mean? When we think of a country's key natural resources, we tend to think in terms of oil or precious minerals; for example, gold in California and coal in West Virginia. But God had something a little different in mind. Honey and milk were staples of the Israelites' diet. They were an agrarian people, and God was promising them a rich land for the grazing of their flocks (remember Moses' primary occupation?) and for growing their vineyards.

The grasses would feed the goats, and the goats would in turn give milk. The good soil would grow the grapes and other vegetation, which would in turn yield wine and the pollen that bees use to make their sweet honey. God was promising to provide a fertile land that would support them and meet their most basic daily needs.

Maybe you're thinking, *Great . . . goats for milk and bees for honey. Just what I don't need. Gold I could always use, but what I'm really after is a job [or a wife, or a buyer for my business, or a cure for an illness]*. Well, I think He's got those things covered too. If God could plunder the Egyptians for gold and prepare a land rich in the very resources His children most needed, don't you believe He can provide equally well for you? The apostle Paul thought so. He said, "My God will meet all your needs according to his glorious riches in Christ Jesus" (Phil. 4:19), and "He who did not spare his own Son, but gave him up for us all—how will he not also, along with him, graciously give us all things?" (Rom. 8:32). If you feel that God is not providing for you, are you walking in His will? Because the God of God's will supplies—and His will never lacks His provision.

When Does God Provide?

Most of us believe that God provides, but we usually feel that His timing is off. He appears perpetually late. If He supplies what His will requires, then *when* does He do that? Let me suggest three situations in which God can be counted on to provide.

First, *He provides when His name and glory are on the line.* He provides when it is clearly about Him—not about us. David wrote, "Not to us, O LORD, not to us but to your name be the glory, because of your love and faithfulness" (Ps. 115:1). God's will is about God—and the quicker we come to understand that, the better off we'll be. Jesus taught His disciples to pray for God's kingdom to come and His will to be done so that His would be the kingdom, the power and the glory forever (see Matt. 6:9-13). God is keen about His own glory, and He can be counted on to provide when His provision points to His glory.

Second, *God provides when we walk in humility before Him.* Moses was a humble man. We are told in Numbers 12:3 that Moses "was a very humble man, more humble than anyone else on the face of the earth." When God first spoke to Moses to call him, Moses responded not with puffed-up pride, but with humility: "Who am I, that I should go to Pharaoh and bring the Israelites out of Egypt?" (Exod. 3:11). Four times Moses pleaded his own unworthiness, and four times God reassured him of His provision. When he claimed that he was not important enough to go before Pharaoh, God said, "Don't worry. I'm sending you there, and you're going to return and worship on this mountain." The second time that Moses said he had no authority, God said, "Tell Pharaoh 'I AM WHO I AM' sent you . . . that should be all the authority you need" (see Exod. 3:14). When he protested a third time that the people might not believe him, God said, "I have some things in mind that will prove what you are saying is from me, things like a staff that turns into a snake and more. You'll see." Finally, when Moses pointed out that he was not much of a public speaker,

God countered, saying, "I'll send Aaron with you, and you can speak through him."

God wants us to respond to him in humility. He knows our limitations. Charles Stanley says it like this: "God knows our limitations and usually will place us in situations that stretch our faith far beyond what we think we can bear. God wants to develop our faith, and in order to do this our faith must be tested."[6]

Finally, *God provides when we come face to face with our shortcomings and insecurities.* When we know how little power or control we have, when we see how meager our resources are, we are primed to trust in God's provision. The bravest person in the world is not the one who buries his or her insecurity, but who faces it head-on. When you and I face our insecurities and plead to God that we don't have what it takes to move forward, He is quick to supply what we need to do His will.

Because God called Moses, God would equip and provide for Moses. His task of delivering the entire Hebrew nation from the bondage of Egypt looked impossible, but an impossible task is just the sort of thing God specializes in.

Even when the task is large, God doesn't necessarily recruit an army. He often begins with a single man or woman. Moses was called to deliver the Israelites from slavery. People with passion throughout history were used by God to change their circumstances and to change hearts. Martin Luther King was called to preach a message of nonviolent resistance in the face of racial injustice, and Rosa Parks was called to take a seat on a Montgomery, Alabama, bus to point out those injustices; Lech Walesa was called to inspire workers in Poland to resist the Communist regime; William Wilberforce was called to speak out in British Parliament against the practice of slave trading when no one else would.

One man or one woman, plus God, does not equal two. One man or one woman, plus God, equals exponential, infinite power. God would prove that through Moses. Moses' job wasn't deliverance; that was God's job. Moses' job was obedience to the God of God's will.

Kelly, my wife, is more of a behind-the-scenes person; but from time to time she is asked to teach in a large group setting. So trusting God outside of her comfort zone has resulted in her faith growing immensely. When she is asked to speak at a women's gathering and doesn't quite feel up to the task, the power of God is her safety net. We were talking one day about an invitation she'd received when she said, "I'm not like you. I can't do this. Pastors are gifted for this. They're used to it. I'm not. I'm a stay-at-home mom." But as we talked, she realized that she was exactly what this assignment called for, and that God is in the business of using willing hearts. God is not looking for eloquent speakers, but faithful stutterers. There's no reason someone with crayons in her purse and Play-Doh under her nails can't be used by God to declare His truth. God doesn't just call the qualified; He qualifies the called. So she said yes, and God did the rest.

And just for the record, pastors get nervous and intimidated too. When I first began leading Breakaway for college friends in my living room, I would get so nervous I had to eat two Pepto-Bismol tablets and pray for an hour before I even came out of my room. I wouldn't make eye contact before it was my time to teach.

I'd just slip in while my roommate was leading worship and sing with the rest of them, eyes closed. I knew that I needed God to the nth degree. I was in way over my head (and still am), but God just smiled and met every need. The secret weapon of every stutterer is placing trust in his or her God who speaks clearly! The next time you feel that God couldn't possibly use you, remember this—you aren't the message; you're just the messenger!

Choose Worship, Not Worry

Finally, the way of God's will is not always easy. Moses encountered resistance and trouble on almost every front after he accepted God's assignment. Pharaoh was not quick to "let God's people go" just because Moses obeyed God and asked. Once the Israelites did leave Egypt, even more trouble ensued. But those troubles were only the by-product of God's will, not the essence of it.

When we try to follow God's will and are met with resistance, we begin to worry that we have misheard Him! The truth is, the tough stuff is part of His plan too. We'll see in chapters 7 and 8 that life can actually get worse in His will before it gets better. Moses even decided to check back in with God to make sure he hadn't misunderstood his instructions:

> Moses returned to the LORD and said, "O LORD, why have you brought trouble upon this people? Is this why you sent me? Ever since I went to Pharaoh to speak in your name, he has brought trouble upon this people, and you have not rescued your people at all" (Exod. 5:22-23).

Smooth sailing is no litmus test for the will of God. Moses did not lead the people out of Egypt for his own pleasure and enjoyment, but for eternal impact and for God's glory. Our aim is the same. We were made for worship, and worship is the essence of God's will. William Temple, the renowned Archbishop of Canterbury, defined worship as "the submission of all our nature to God. It is the quickening of conscience by his holiness, the nourishment of the mind with his truth, the purifying of the imagination of his beauty, the opening of the heart to his love, the surrender of the will to his purpose."[7]

God's will moves us toward worship, because His will is about Him, not about us. Worship is our way and our end, our traveling companion and our destination. Don't confuse the by-products of God's will—especially the negative ones—with the end and essence of His will: worship. The plan of God for us is not short-term ease, but long-term impact. We are tools in His hands so that the glory might be His and His alone. The "who" precedes the "what." Only when we are led by the God of God's will do we know when to *bailamos* and when to *vamos*!

For Further Thought and Discussion

1. Why does a discussion about God's will need to begin with God instead of you?
2. Moses described God as compassionate and caring. What words have you found to best describe God?
3. Why do we need to clearly understand that God provides?

4. What do you need Him to provide right now?

5. How does the truth that God's will never lacks God's supply help our faith?

Notes

1. *Merriam-Webster's Dictionary* online, s.v. "compassion." http://www.merriam-webster.com/dictionary/compassion.

2. V. Raymond Edman, *The Disciplines of Life* (Minneapolis, MN: World Wide Publications, 1948), p. 54.

3. Beth Moore, message given during a Living Proof Ministries Tuesday Night Bible Study, 2009.

4. Ed Reese, "The Life and Ministry of George Meuller," *The Christian Hall of Fame* series (Knoxville, TN: Reese Publications, nd). www.truthfulwords.org/biography/muller.txt.

5. Douglas K. Stuart, "An Exegetical and Theological Exposition of Holy Scripture," *The New American Commentary*, vol. 2, *Exodus* (Nashville, TN: Broadman & Holman, 2007), p. 124.

6. Charles F. Stanley, *Landmines in the Path of the Believer* (Nashville, TN: Thomas Nelson, 2007), pp. 66-67.

7. William Temple, *Readings in St. John's Gospel* (Harrisburg, PA: Morehouse Publications, 1985).

5

THREE ORANGES: GOD'S WILL FOR EVERYONE

Late in the evening of April 14, 1912, the unsinkable ocean liner Titanic struck an iceberg and sank to the bottom of the sea, claiming the lives of 1,523 of the 2,228 men, women and children aboard. Survivor stories provide a wealth of information about what took place during the last few minutes of the ill-fated ship's journey, and these tales are peppered with heroism and selfishness, wisdom and folly.

Among the many wealthy passengers sailing on Titanic's maiden voyage was Major Arthur Godfrey Peuchen, who survived while 11 other millionaires died. Peuchen remembered returning to his stateroom and stuffing three oranges in his pockets as the ship was being evacuated. He left cash, securities and jewelry worth more than $300,000—but he took three oranges. In the cataclysmic last moments of Titanic's voyage, Peuchen saw with great clarity the difference between essentials and nonessentials. He chose to carry with him the basics— just three oranges—knowing that they could provide life to him or to someone else while they were waiting to be rescued.[1]

As we seek to know the will of God, are we focusing on what could truly give life to our souls, or are we simply looking for another toy to add to life's toy box? Can we appreciate the value of the basics—the "oranges"—over the more glamorous aspects of His will?

While God has a specific will for each person, He also has a general will for every man, woman and child. God's general will is the same for everyone, no burning bush required. It is a matter of right and wrong, not right or left. For example, the Ten Commandments, sexual purity, honesty, personal holiness and kindness to others are His will for everyone. By following His general will, we lay a foundation for His specific will to be built upon. It's not rocket science; the way to find God's specific will is to do His general will. We could think of His general will like Peuchen's oranges—essential, life-giving, ordinary and applicable to all.

Three Things We Know Are God's Will

Knowing God's will doesn't require memorizing a formula. Instead it involves living a process that is our life's journey. But even so, a foundation for knowing His will exists for every man or woman regardless of his or her vocation, personality or gifting. In fact, you may be encouraged to discover that you already know far more of the path than you realize!

Three things reliably fall into the category of God's general will for us, and they undergird every word of this book. They're rooted in *His* book, and without them, nothing else I say will be of much use at all. If we can only get these three things right, we'll be grounded and off to a solid start in knowing God's specific will. The foundation must be laid before the building can be built. So let's consider these three "oranges" before we go any further.

Orange 1: Relationship

God's plan for your life and my life begins with relationship. Jesus is the very embodiment of God's desire to know us, and the only way for us to know Him (see John 14:6). All through the Scriptures, God is seen reaching out to man, inviting him into relationship. In the Garden of Eden, God walked in the cool of the day with Adam and Eve; in Exodus, He took Moses from his wanderings to the tent of meeting; through the Old Testament prophets, He called a wayward people to restored relationship; and the psalms sing of the One who is the establishing rock of this relationship. In the New Testament, God came even closer with the birth of His Son who would be both redeemer and friend to man; and the gospel story ends in Revelation with a city of jewels where God and man will live forever in glorious fellowship. All 66 books of the Bible call for and celebrate relationship—a divine relationship based on identity, not on activity.

Our relationship with God does not stem from a "do" but a "Who." We don't act or work our way into relationship with God; He lovingly extends the offer of relationship to us through His Son, Jesus Christ. His identity as our Father precedes and makes possible our identity as His children. In the same way, I don't "father" my children to *become* their parent; I father my children because I *am* their parent. They are who they are because I am who I am.

I did not always understand this. I grew up thinking that my connection to God was based mostly upon my actions. I believed that if I behaved in a certain way, I could get closer to Him, or conversely, that my poor behavior put distance between us. I thought somehow that it all depended upon me. I imagined that if I performed reasonably well in comparison to others, God would be pleased. This misguided belief reduced my life to a lackluster PG-13 performance that could never satisfy a holy God or establish a true relationship with Him. The idea of sacrifice was foreign to me; a vibrant love for God was for those who had taken the "religion thing" a little too far. I saw life as a walk on the fairway, with par as the goal. I thought vibrant believers were cut from a different kind of cloth than ordinary me.

But it is not our efforts that unlock heaven; it is Christ's death and resurrection. We all have made mistakes, but more than that, we have all deliberately chosen to ignore God's commands and fulfill our own desires instead. This walking away from God is called sin. As James 4:17 says, "Anyone, then, who knows the good he ought to do and doesn't do it, sins."

Our culture scoffs at the idea of sin. We call our disobedience "no big deal," because "everybody makes mistakes." But in God's eyes our sin is big stuff. It's serious. It's so serious to a holy God that blood, death and sacrifice were required to reverse the curse of sin. Thankfully, God Himself stepped in (enter Jesus, stage right) with the necessary sacrifice, offering a grace-filled, permanent remedy for our sin. Jesus Christ lived the life we couldn't—a life completely without sin—and paid the price for us, providing the blood, death and sacrifice required by God. That's how our sins can be forgiven and our relationship with a holy God secured.

By placing our faith in Jesus Christ's sacrificial death for our sin, we are saved from God's wrath. Jesus didn't die just for "people in general." He died for me. He died for you.

Our relationship with God as a son or daughter begins when we trust Jesus for salvation. That is God's will for us. How do I know? His Word tells me:

> This is good, and pleases God our Savior, who wants all men to be saved and to come to a knowledge of the truth. For there is one God and one mediator between God and men, the man Christ Jesus, who gave himself as a ransom for all men—the testimony given in the proper time (1 Tim. 2:3-6).

This might sound clear to those of you who are "well churched," but it wasn't to me. I did not grow up going to church. Before I came to know Christ, I tried to balance the scales with good deeds to outweigh my sins. But that was not relationship. That was not being; that was doing. I didn't have a clue that God wanted me to be in a relationship with Him.

The summer between my sophomore and junior years in high school, I worked at a supermarket, sacking groceries. There was a checker there that I thought was really cute, so I made a bet with her about a football game, saying that whichever one of us lost would take the other to dinner. I lost, which actually meant I won. I took her to get some Mexican food, and we began dating. She was a Christian; I was not. She shouldn't have even been dating me, but she did.

One night, she went with my future Christian friends to a Michael W. Smith concert, and something about that evening compelled her to share Christ with me on the phone. I realized as I listened to her that I was headed for hell. I started crying on the phone. Later that week we went to her youth minister's house, and he explained how to have a relationship with Christ. I told him that if I did what he suggested—trust Christ for my salvation—I would lose all my friends. Regardless, I knew I needed Christ in my life, so I bowed my head and prayed something like this: "Lord, I know I have sinned so many times. I trust Your death on the cross to be the payment for my sin. I ask You to forgive my sins and wash me clean." (If you have never taken that step, I encourage you to pray those words from your heart right now.) In Romans, Paul says, "If you confess with your mouth, 'Jesus is Lord,' and believe in your heart that God raised him from the dead, you will be saved" (Rom. 10:9).

That night my life was changed for eternity, but it took some time for my lifestyle to catch up with my new heart. I "rode the fence" for most of my junior year—going out drinking with my old buddies during the week, and going to church on Sunday.

Finally, I went with a group from my girlfriend's church to a high school week at Glorieta, New Mexico, and got it straightened out for good. I remember crying as I watched my friends walk down the aisle to pray or talk to a counselor at the conclusion of the service. For a long time I thought that "I Have Decided to Follow Jesus" was just a camp song. That week I learned it was a choice. These days, lots of people imagine that I was reared in a church-going home, or that there were other pastors in my family. I didn't . . . and there weren't.

Even today my high school friends can't believe I'm a pastor, and my church friends can't believe I was a partyer. But thankfully, God initiated a relationship with me during those years based on His love, and not my performance. That was the beginning step for me in knowing His will for my life. He meant for me to be His, and now I am.

Simply put, relationship is the bedrock of all that follows. It is an essential—an "orange"—of God's will. What is your relationship with God like? Have you trusted Christ for forgiveness and become a child of God? I'm not asking if you mentally assent that Jesus Christ is the Son of God. I am asking if you have trusted Him as your Savior, and if you've depended upon Him and Him alone to reconcile you with God. If not, why wait? You'll never figure out what God wants you to do with your life until you allow Him to change who you are. Being must precede doing, and being begins with relationship.

Orange 2: Growth

The second "orange" of God's general will for His children is growth. He wants each of us to be in a vibrant, growing relationship with Jesus Christ. This growth is not just for the exceptional "Navy Seal" special forces-type Christian, but also for every son or daughter of God. We imagine that the "Seals" have a special thing going with God that the rest of us aren't privy to—but nothing could be further from the truth. Growth isn't reserved for those of us with "pastor" printed on our business card; we pastors don't have a red phone under glass that connects us directly to heaven. We grow like you do—one step of obedience at a time. Growth is God's general will for all of His children, not just a select few. Paul plainly told the church of Thessalonica, "It is God's will that you should be sanctified" (1 Thess. 4:3), clearly stating that God desires us to grow in our personal holiness.

Not only does God desire for us to grow, but we also desire it. As believers, the Holy Spirit lives in us and serves as a compass to point us God-ward to growth according to His values. Our desires begin to change, making us long for holiness, not for sin. Growth does not come from a laundry list of rule keeping or list making or Bible reading or church attendance. It comes from a new set of values lived from the inside out. Spiritual growth stems from changed values. When we value God more than some otherworldly thing, growth occurs as a result of that judgment. As we value Christ more than the urgencies of the day, growth will come.

Do I value Christ above all else? If I do, then those "spiritual" activities that used to be "have-tos" will instead become "want-tos," and I will begin to respond to God not out of legalism but out of love. When I judge Him to be more important than anything else, I grow. When I say, "Jesus, I value You more than three hours of mindless television," I grow. When I say, "Jesus, I value You more than the opinions of my friends," I grow. The amount of worth I place on knowing Jesus determines how genuinely I will relate to Him. The process loop goes something like this: Valuing Christ highly results in a desire to hear from Him, and the more I hear from Him, the more I value Him. Simply put, value precedes action. So together with the first "orange" of relationship, I add the second "orange" of growth. No doubt, no debate, God desires all of us to be in a growing relationship with Him—and no matter your place in life, He makes that available to us all.

What does this growing relationship look like? It means that I can visit a relative or a friend in a cancer ward and value Christ above knowing the answers to questions about illness and death. It means that in a conversation that turns confrontational, I can value Christ above the resolution of tension. It means that I can place a higher value on a mission trip with my family than a grand vacation. Growth stems from value. As you walk out the door to do life today, deliberately state your intent to value Christ over whatever else your heart may desire. When you see something that you naturally place a high value on, say, "Jesus, I love You more."

I did this for the first time at a luxury hotel in Dallas, where I was speaking at a conference. I saw the ornate lobby and my beautiful room, and I said, "Jesus, I love You more than wealth or comfort." When I saw my name tag that read "speaker," I said, "Jesus, I love You more than notoriety." When I was greeted by welcoming friends and strangers, I said again in my heart, "Jesus, I love You more than the attentions of men." By declaring the higher value of my relationship to Christ and my love for Him, I was able to fight the twin temptations of envy and pride. Stating the value I place on Christ helped to put those things in perspective, and growth stemmed from acting on that value. It's pretty simple: Growth stems from value. The more I discover and profess the indescribable value of the Savior, the more my love for Him grows.

What have you incorrectly valued that might be hampering your growth in Christ? Let me suggest a few competitors. A relationship? A job? Your performance? A special gift or skill that you possess? Growth will not occur in that area until your values are rightly aligned. Could you say today in truth, "Jesus, I love You more than _____"? C. S. Lewis famously assessed our wrongly placed values when he said:

> We are half-hearted creatures, fooling about with drink and sex and ambition when infinite joy is offered us, like an ignorant child who wants to go on making mud pies in a slum because he cannot imagine what is meant by the offer of a holiday at the sea. We are far too easily pleased.[2]

When you rightly value God, you can release your grip on things of lesser value. Your mind can be renewed to love differently. God can enlarge your heart, and teach you to love Him more. True growth comes from rightly valuing Christ above all else. When we do this, time spent with Him is joy, and pursuit of Him is a happy discipline. Look at whatever impedes your progress, dead in the eye, and say, "Jesus, I love You more." This love will find its way to action as your Bible becomes a prized possession and your prayers become conversations with God instead of perfunctory repeats.

Orange 3: Impact

Impact is the final essential, the final "orange" in God's general will for His children. Relationship and growth make a strong one-two punch, but there's more. God means for His children to make an impact in this world—and we long for impact too. None of us wants to be forgotten, passed by, without a legacy. We want our lives to count for something. We don't want to be mourned for a day and forgotten for a lifetime! Perhaps this is why for centuries kings and statesmen have commanded statues to be erected in their honor. They don't want to be forgotten.

Thankfully, God also wants our lives to count—for Him and for His kingdom. I can unequivocally say that God's will for your life and mine is that we make an impact for His kingdom. Married, single, old, young, rich or poor, we are meant to lead lives of impact. Dr. Rick Rigsby has a great way of putting it: "Leaving an impression is one thing," he says, "but leaving a lasting impact is another."[3] Living with impact for the kingdom is living in a way that draws others to Christ. We leave an indelible mark for eternity when our lives point to the Someone who is greater than all; when we are anchored securely to His great renown. "We have this hope as an anchor for the soul," said the writer of Hebrews, "firm and secure" (Heb. 6:19).

Because we desire to make an impact, and because Christ is the anchor that holds us fast, we achieve a legacy by obediently positioning ourselves to be used by Him while stepping out in faith. Lives that are anchored in Christ are lives marked by service to the poor, love shown to the unlovable, faith shared and gifts used. You don't have to be "big time" to make a big difference! Just step out in faith and serve.

As Christians . . . We Help People . . . Go to Heaven

After Major Peuchen returned to his Titanic stateroom and filled his pockets with three oranges, he escaped the sinking

82

ship with his own life, together with other survivors. What are you and I to do after we establish a relationship with God through Christ, begin to grow in Him, and, anchored in Christ, seek to live lives of impact? What's the goal or purpose for these three aspects of God's will? Is it just to bring those less fortunate "up a notch" by acts of service? Surely Christ didn't give His life so that we might "buy the world a Coke and keep it company" as the jingle goes. There has to be more than that. Many well-meaning organizations do wonderful things in the name of kindness or social justice. But Christians do it in Jesus' name: "I tell you the truth," Jesus said, "anyone who gives you a cup of water in my name because you belong to Christ will certainly not lose his reward" (Mark 9:41). Let's dig deeper into making a lasting impact.

I once heard Pastor Ken Whitten say a sentence that reshaped my thoughts on impact. He said, "The goal of the Bible is not to make the earth a better place to go to hell from." Whoa. Rewind. Let me hear that again. "The goal of the Bible is not to make the earth a better place to go to hell from." This statement doesn't belittle good works or discourage those who would seek to better society through kindness or acts of service. It simply implies that eternity is paramount, and our primary aim should be to make sure we keep eternity front and center. In the gospel of Matthew, Jesus said, "In the same way, let your light shine before men, that they may see your good deeds and praise your Father in heaven" (Matt. 5:16).

In other words, all the earthly good that we might do should have a heavenly motivation and perspective. Lasting impact is more that just meeting a social or physical need.

Christians should most definitely strive to meet the physical needs of the poor, but it doesn't end there. We give a cup of cold water, but we give it in Jesus' name—meaning, for His sake and purpose (see Matt. 10:42; Mark 9:41). The cold water is a temporary tool to open the heart to an eternal truth. Our lives should be about sharing the good news of relationship with Jesus Christ, because eternity without Him is a terrible, permanent sentence. Here's our statement of impact: As Christians . . . we help people . . . go to heaven. Each section of this sentence plays a vital role.

As Christians . . .

Let's begin to break that sentence down: Our goal . . . as Christians . . . is to help people . . . go to heaven. Our service as Christians rests upon the foundation of our identity in Christ. His power always accompanies His will—remember? And any impact we have will come from His power. This means that in terms of lasting impact, my personality, my gifts and my experience are secondary to my identity in Christ. As a point of personal confession, this means a lot to me. I am often tempted to trust in my own abilities and rely on my winsomeness over His. "In Gregg we trust" is written on a lot of the currency I try to spend; I have accomplished a lot with a gregarious, engaging style and a quick story. (And I've gotten into my share of trouble with those same "assets"!) As Scottish novelist George MacDonald said, "In whatever man does without God, he must fail miserably or succeed more miserably."[4]

Second, as Christians, Christ has forgiven us. That compels us to make an impact (see 2 Cor. 5:14). How could we receive all that we have and sit on the bench when such an important game is being played? Second Corinthians 1:4 says that we ourselves are comforted "so that we can comfort those in any trouble with the comfort we ourselves have received from God." Often, a lack of impact in our lives stems from not realizing the impact of Christ's salvation. Passive Christians are those who have not spent time discovering all that God has done for them. Their thought is that Jesus changes morality, and where you spend Sunday morning, but not your view of the world. The cross moves us from darkness to light, not from shadow to shade. We are new creations in Christ (see 2 Cor. 5:17). Therefore, in His power—changed by Him—we step out in faith to make a difference.

Scotty Sanders is a modern example of this. She grew up in a pastor's home but drifted from the general will of God. Ultimately, she became a singer in Las Vegas and then married Doug Sanders, one of the most famous golfers of his day. Private jets, mansions and famous friends like Frank Sinatra were her life. Eventually, Scotty recognized her life was about her, not Christ. As she woke up to what Christ had truly done in her heart, that He was about more than her just being a good little girl, she returned to Christ. As she discovered Him by living His general will, His specific will rose like cream to the top.

Experimenting with her heart of compassion, she began serving the poor. Today, 20 years later, Scotty lives in a low-income apartment complex, usually with a troubled teen sleeping on the couch for a couple of days. She also is the director of our church's local mission efforts to the needy. Life is immeasurably different for Scotty in regard to joy and purpose. She serves in Christ's strength, yielding each day to Him. She serves because of the change He has made in her. Her once-lukewarm faith is now white hot as she lives with purpose and impact.

We Help People . . .

Christians should be the most helpful people in any community. We are compelled to love the poor by clothing, teaching and feeding them. Practically speaking, that means Christian students should look around the lunchroom for someone sitting alone and ask, "Would you like to sit with me?" It means that the clothes in your closet that don't get worn but are still in good shape should be on someone else's back. I don't mind at all returning home from a mission trip with an empty suitcase.

A word of caution: If you only minister to those less fortunate than you, you can start to feel a false sense of impact—a world in which you are never socially at risk and always praised for your compassion. Everyone is for feeding the homeless on a Saturday morning, but you are considered a fanatic to verbally share with your boss on Monday the change Christ has brought to your life. Of course, it is important to minister to the poor, but God's will is that we would impact the homeless person *and* the boss. The real risk comes when we minister to a peer or to someone higher on the social "food chain" than us. Now there is a risk, because there we stand to lose status or respect because of our beliefs. So often we drift to a safe place of defining impact as raising a person's physical status for a few hours.

Not every need is physical, nor is every needy person poor. As humans we are physical, social, emotional and spiritual; therefore, we have needs in each area. The discerning impact player sees the area of need and steps in to help. We help people in various ways. The teen needs friends, and so sports and activities are often the way to their heart. The married couple needs to decrease the "ice in the house," so a listening ear can show them the possibilities of a marriage under His watch. The down and out are not the only ones in need; there are plenty of up and out-ers too.

The point is, as Christians, we help people's short-term needs but we don't stop there. Short-term help allows us to take the next (and scariest) step of opening our mouths to share the claims of Jesus. It is far easier to open your wallet, your closet or your kitchen than to open your heart and mouth. As a result, we stop too early, satisfied to only make this earth "a better place to go to hell from."

Christians take some hard (and not always undeserved) hits for being unhelpful to those in physical need. The Body of believers will always be a target for accusations of hypocrisy and wrongdoing. Believe me, as pastor of a large church, I've heard my share. But let me ask you this: How many soup kitchens or pantries or shelters or hospitals in your town have no church affiliation whatsoever? Seen any "Soup Kitchens of the Pop Star" or "Hollywood Starlets for the Homeless" in your city lately? Neither have I. My city is filled with hospitals named after saints and denominations. But how many atheist hospitals can you name? If you remove Christianity from history, you have just removed an overwhelming amount of help to society. The history of most aid organizations can be traced back to Christianity, or at least to one Christian devoted to helping people.

Step one: Realize what Christ has done for you.

Step two: Identify the need and meet it.

But be aware that this help is not the end. It is a tool to discuss their ultimate need: a relationship with Jesus.

Go to Heaven . . .

As Christians . . . we help people. That's a good place to stop, right? Well, lots of folks *do* stop there, but God doesn't mean for us to. You may be fearful to take the next step or overly mindful of risking offense. But Christians . . . should be helping people . . . go to heaven.

Sure, there are times when we "plant seeds" that someone else will water; but the ultimate goal of our help should be eternal, not temporal. First, we must meet the felt need. But we shouldn't stop there. We should take the risk and say, "I helped you today because Jesus has helped me so much. He wants to help you, too, more than this coat or sack of groceries can. Can I tell you about Jesus, and how you can know Him?" If he or she says a big fat no, then say thank you and that you will pray for him or her. (Then do it.) If the person says yes, then the aid you gave has prepared him or her to hear more about why you helped. Tell the story of how you trusted Jesus, and invite the person to do the same.

One of the most vibrant ministries of our church is a center with a clothes closet and a food pantry. With Scotty Sanders at the wheel, this center has won local honors for its above-and-beyond service. One award declared our ministry to be the best food pantry in the city, secular or religious.

What happens at the clothes closet and food pantry? A church member greets folks who come to the center and helps them shop with dignity for what they need, and then he or she helps the person assemble a bag of groceries. Another volunteer shares the plan of salvation. Some folks say, "Thanks but no thanks," and that's okay. But others—more than 1,000 people a year—enter the kingdom of God because someone demonstrated the love of God to them through temporal things and then told them how they could be eternally saved. Tens of thousands are in heaven today because before they took their last breath on this earth, a Christian helped them and loved them enough to tell them why.

Some people just want to preach and some just want to serve. We need both serving *and* preaching! The combination of the two brings real, lasting impact!

> Suppose a brother or sister is without clothes and daily food. If one of you says to him, "Go, I wish you well; keep warm and well fed," but does nothing about his physical needs, what good is it? In the same way, faith by itself, if it is not accompanied by action, is dead (Jas. 2:15-17).

My wife drives an SUV with two kids in the back seat and Cheerios scattered on the floorboard, fitting the soccer mom persona. But in the center console reside several zip-lock bags with a can of Vienna sausages, peanut butter crackers and a pamphlet that shares the gospel. When we see a homeless person, and we often do, my son rolls down the window and hands the bag to the person. We have yet to see someone drop to his or her knees in prayer—most just want cash—but the person says thanks. Our first goal is to help, but we also want to teach our children something about ministering to the physical and spiritual needs of people.

As believers, we can have a far deeper impact than a compassionate movie star or a government program. I'm so grateful for the social awareness and generosity we see in our world, but Christians have even more to offer. We are not serving to relieve guilt over our blessings but to transfer our blessings to another in such a way that they see Jesus working through us. More than a better earth, we desire a filled heaven. Get creative and take a step of faith. Realize what Christ has done, and in that strength, help someone in need and, most importantly, tell him or her why you did.

God's will for everyone is that we would know Him through His Son, Jesus Christ. It's His will that we would grow in our relationship with Him, and that our lives would have lasting, eternal impact. Relationship . . . growth . . . and impact—those are the "three oranges" of God's general will for us. You have to make it off the sinking ship to enjoy the rest of life. You have to grasp the essentials, or nothing else matters. By discovering these three essentials of God's will, you establish a foundation upon which the specific will of God for your life can rest. As C. S. Lewis put it, "You can't get second things by putting them first; you can get second things only by putting first things first."[5]

For Further Reflection and Discussion

1. How is God's general will different from His specific will?
2. What is your big challenge to fill the blank in the sentence "Jesus, I love You more than_____"? What would your spouse or close friend say your big challenge is?

3. Which of these three "oranges"—relationship, growth or impact—is most lacking in your life? Which one needs your attention the most?

4. Are you helping people go to heaven? If not, what holds you back?

5. What can you or your family do to help people go to heaven?

Notes

1. Marshall Everett, ed., *Wreck and Sinking of the Titanic: The Ocean's Greatest Disaster* (L. H. Walter, 1912), p. 106. http://www.archive.org/stream/wrecksinkingofti00neiluoft/wrecksinkingofti00neiluoft_djvu.txt.

2. C. S. Lewis, "The Weight of Glory," original sermon delivered in the church of St. Mary the Virgin, Oxford, June 8, 1942. Published in *Theology*, November 1941.

3. Dr. Rick Rigsby, *Lessons from a Third Grade Dropout* (Nashville, TN: Thomas Nelson, 2006), p. 1.

4. George MacDonald, *Unspoken Sermons,* series 2 (Charleston, SC: BiblioBazaar, 2006), p. 248.

5. C. S. Lewis, "First and Second Things," quoted in Walter Hooper, ed., *C.S. Lewis: Readings for Meditation and Reflection* (New York: Harper Collins, 1996), p. 14.

6

The Two Hurdles of God's Will

As this book is being written, the world-record time for the 100-meter dash is held by Usain Bolt, a Jamaican sprinter . . . but records are made to be broken. Bolt posted his 9.58-second record time at the World Athletics Championships, bettering his own previous score by just over a tenth of a second. The 100-meter dash is about quick acceleration and pure, unhindered speed; the record holder for this race is frequently referred to as the fastest man alive.

In contrast, the record for the 110-meter hurdles is held by Dayron Robles of Cuba, at 12.87 seconds—a difference of more than 3 seconds over the dash, which is an eternity in "sprint time." But it's not the extra 10 meters that slows the pace—it's the hurdles. Ten 3.5-foot hurdles are staggered throughout the 110-meter distance, slowing the runners' pace even if each one is cleared perfectly!

Hurdles can impede us in finding and doing the will of God, too. Moses, our "guide" in discovering the God of God's will, drew near to the burning bush on the backside of nowhere and heard God speak to him there. But as soon as Moses heard what God had to say, he encountered two significant hurdles—and those same things can become barriers for you and me.

What did the God of compassion say? He told Moses He had seen the misery of His people, and He had a plan to deliver them—a plan that included Moses:

> I have indeed seen the misery of my people in Egypt. I have heard them crying out because of their slave drivers, and I am concerned about their suffering. So I have come down to rescue them from the hand of the Egyptians. . . . So now, go. I am sending you to Pharaoh to bring my people the Israelites out of Egypt (Exod. 3:7-8,10).

At this point, however, Moses the shepherd turned into Moses the sheepish. He said to God, "Who am I, that I should go to Pharaoh and bring the Israelites out of Egypt?" (Exod. 3:11). God assured Moses that He would go with him. Then Moses voiced another concern: "Suppose I go to the Israelites and say to them, 'The God of your fathers has sent me to you,' and they ask me, 'What is his name?' Then what shall I tell them?" (v. 13).

Again, God reassured Moses: "Say to the Israelites, 'The LORD, the God of your fathers—the God of Abraham, the God of Isaac and the God of Jacob—has sent me to you'" (v. 15). Then God instructed Moses on exactly what he was to say and do, and what would happen when he did! But Moses wasn't done objecting. He saved his two tallest "hurdles" for last. He first asked, "What if they do not believe me or listen to me, and say, 'The LORD did not appear to you'?" (Exod. 4:1).

What if they don't believe me or listen to me? What if they doubt that I really saw God or heard His voice? The first hurdle in knowing and following God's will involves "they." Who are "they"? They're the remarkably ambiguous but powerful voices of doubt and dissent. *They* are the unidentified ones whose opinions we fear and whose favor we'd like to have. Someone has said that the desire for the approval of others can cause us to spend money we don't have, to buy things we don't need, to impress people we don't even know! *They* say what is the currently fashionable or acceptable. *They* are an unnamed powerful influencer. "They" can be intimidating, can't they?

Hurdle #1: What Will "They" Say?

Moses had a "they" problem. "They" presented a hurdle to him in getting on with the will of God. Have you ever wondered what "they" might say about God's will for your life? How "they" might react if you were to take a step out in faith and follow Him? Or, what would "they" say if you insisted you'd heard directly from God? Moses was worried enough about "they" that even in the very presence of God, he hesitated.

A behavioral study was done years ago by a university professor that demonstrated the remarkable power of "they." This professor got a group of 15 people together and handed them cards with one line and three lines, and asked them which of the three lines matched the length of the first line. The correct answer was "line B"; but as each person in sequence incorrectly (and purposely) answered, "line A," the number of subsequent people who would answer correctly diminished even though they knew that "B" was correct! Participants gave the wrong answer because they were influenced by the cumulative power of "they."[1]

The first hurdle in knowing and embracing God's will is concern over what "they" will say. Living for the Lord will definitely raise the eyebrows of some, but as I've said many times, you wouldn't worry about what people think of you if you knew how seldom they thought of you! Believe it or not, we're not "top of mind" material for "they" 24-7. Why live for the approval of others when you are not even on the front burner of their thoughts? However, God does have you on His mind: "How precious to me are your thoughts, O God! How vast is the sum of them! Were I to count them, they would outnumber the grains of sand" (Ps. 139:17-18). He thinks of you all the time.

When I was a soon-to-be high school senior, I went with my peers to the New Mexico summer camp I mentioned in the previous chapter. I've since spoken at countless camps across the country, but that one summer was my only experience "in the pew" as a camper myself. It was a great week—a significant one in my life. The afternoon before the bus trip home, my youth minister, Dennis Perry, assembled those of us about to be seniors and asked us all a question: "Would you like to know what I really think of you?" Wow. My first thought was, *Uh, only if it's good.*

His goal was not to exact sweet youth minister revenge on us for our camp shenanigans, although we might have deserved it. What he wanted to do was shine light on the blind spots of our lives so that we might grow in Christ in the coming year. So, we assembled for an hour I'll never forget. As he went around the room, speaking to each senior, some tears were shed and some pride got broken, but a ton of loving truth was heard as well.

My stomach dropped when he got to the "please like me" kid named Gregg Matte. First, he encouraged me before my peers by conveying to me how much I had grown in the eight months since I'd prayed with him at his house, asking Jesus to forgive my sin. I was glad for that. But his last words to me revealed a hurdle I knew I struggled with. His words were dead on: "Gregg, God could really use you if you quit worrying about what everyone else thought of you."

I nodded in affirmation, and then he went on to the next kid. But what a life changer that moment was for me! The truth can hurt, but the same hurt can also heal. I still think back on his words today when I'm tempted to seek the approval of men, or to live for "they" and not for "Thee." It takes courage to tune out the "they" in our lives. True bravery is facing your fears together with the Lord and walking with Him beyond them. Don't mask your fears or avoid your anxieties; face them in the Lord and say, "God, I don't care what they say. I'm not following 'they.' I'm following 'Thee.'"

Some of the worst decisions of our life are made for "them." We may even make choices to please or impress people we will not know 10 years from now. We mistakenly worry about pleasing "them" rather than following "Thee." Moses asked God, "What if they say it's not true? What if they say I never heard from You?" It's ironic that Moses feared "their" doubts when he stood in the very presence of God. But "they" can quickly cause us to doubt what we know is true—even when the Truth stands before us and calls us by name. Moses knew that the Lord's appearance was real. He saw the bush and heard the voice. But his hurdle remained. The doubts of others can make the truth seem false. *Moses, God could really use you if you quit worrying about what everyone else thought of you.*

God Demonstrates His Surpassing Power

Mercifully, God did not condemn Moses for his doubts. Instead, He demonstrated to Moses His mighty power so that the specter of "they" became small in comparison with the splendor of God.

"What is that in your hand?" God asked Moses.

"A staff," Moses replied.

"Throw it on the ground," God commanded him. And when he did, the staff became a snake.

"Reach out your hand and take it by the tail," God said. Moses did, and the snake became a staff again (see Exod. 4:1-5).

Moses had a staff in his hand because Moses was a shepherd. Shepherds weren't favored in Egypt, however. They were detested. When Joseph's brothers arrived in Egypt to escape the famine of their homeland, Joseph instructed them that all shepherds are detestable to the Egyptians (see Gen. 46:33-34). Shepherds were viewed as the lowest rung of society in Egypt, and Moses knew it. But God told him to take his shepherd's staff with him to see Pharaoh, and then to use it to achieve His purposes!

Do you know what snakes symbolized in ancient Egypt? Power. In fact, Egyptian soldiers wore headdresses adorned by the cobra, representing the serpent god Apep, the destroyer. So when Moses' staff turned into a snake and he seized it by the tail, his action would say in effect to God's people, "I've got Egypt and its little-*g* gods by the tail!" Moses' willingness to act as God commanded would demonstrate the belief that his life-giving God had power over Pharaoh's destroying, avenging gods. It would be something like striding into the oval office with your hands around the neck of a bald eagle—the symbol of power of the United States of America—and then glaring at the president! God said, "This . . . is so that they may believe that the LORD, the God of their fathers—the God of Abraham, the God of Isaac, and the God of Jacob—has appeared to you" (Exod. 4:5). Even in his lowly shepherd's clothing, carrying his simple staff, Moses possessed more power in his right hand than all the gods and magicians of Pharaoh's court combined. Nothing like the power of God to put the voice of "they" in the proper place!

Then God gave Moses two more supernatural signs of His presence and authority—almost like a plan B and plan C. God knew the hardness of Pharaoh's heart. He knew one simple sign would not be enough to convince him to let the Israelites go. And He would use the hardness of Pharaoh's heart to display His power to His own people *and* to the Egyptians. So he further instructed Moses, "Put your hand inside your cloak" (Exod. 4:6), and Moses did. When he took it out, his hand was white with leprosy!

"Now put it back in," God told him. And when Moses did, and withdrew it again, it was restored.

Leprosy was a dread disease that rendered its victim unclean according to Jewish law. Unclean, the Jew could not be in God's presence to worship Him. God's demonstration of sickness and healing, of Moses' hand concealed and revealed, showed His power to bring His people out and make their worship acceptable in His sight. Their life among the Egyptians as slaves had made them unfit for worship—unclean—but God was able to cleanse them and bring them into His presence unspotted and free.

God's third verifying demonstration for Moses—His plan C, if you will—was no less dramatic than the first two. "If they do not believe you or pay attention to the first miraculous sign," God told Moses, "they may believe the second. But if they do not believe these two signs or listen to you, take some water from the Nile and pour it on the dry ground. The water you take from the river will become blood on the ground" (Exod. 4:8-9).

The Egyptians equated the Nile River with life. It was their water supply, their "divine" source of life and sustenance. They congregated around the Nile. They revered and depended upon the Nile, and the Israelites knew it. But Moses would dip into the Nile River and turn the water he drew out of it into blood, showing that the supernatural, life-giving power of Yahweh surpassed any other source of power. To Israel this little demonstration would say that the Egyptians' power source was "owned" by the God of Abraham, Isaac and Jacob. It was the equivalent of a seven-foot NBA superstar slam-dunking over a five-foot, middle school point guard! (By the way, when Pharaoh saw this mini-demo, he should have learned his lesson . . . but ultimately the entire Nile River would run with blood as he hardened his heart against Israel and her God.)

Together these three signs gave proof of God's power to accomplish His purpose. Remember, His will is always accompanied by His power. The staff that became a snake and then a staff again; the leprous hand that was concealed, then revealed whole and restored; and the water of the Nile turned to blood—all of these miracles conveyed His power. They also reveal more to us in the pages of the New Testament. The gospel is right there in Exodus: the wooden staff of the shepherd Moses foreshadows the wooden cross of the Good Shepherd, Jesus Christ, whose heel was bruised by the serpent Satan, but who crushed the head of the Deceiver and won the victory over sin and death. This same cross is the vehicle for our cleansing from the "leprosy" of sin, making us pure and acceptable in the sight of God. And the blood that was shed on the cross by Jesus Christ is our lifeline and the power that sustains us in life and in death.

You wouldn't worry about what "they" might say with that kind of power on your side, would you? You wouldn't constantly check your approval numbers among men if you knew the power of Almighty God was behind His plan for your life, would you? In light of His power, the hurdle of "they" seems insignificant.

"Gregg," my high school youth minister said, "God could really use you if you quit worrying about what everyone else thought of you." His words were well timed and true. The world's opinion is no match for the power of the God of God's will. I've discovered since that day that it is actually easier to please God than man. Man is fickle, God is stable, and so I can clearly understand what kinds of "oranges" please Him.

Hurdle #2: Spectator or Participant?

Once God's demonstration of power got Moses over that first hurdle, he quickly faced the second one: Would he be a spectator or a participant in God's great plan of deliverance? Moses had hardly acknowledged the miracles he saw before he pleaded with God for a nice bleacher seat: "O, Lord, please send someone else to do it." In other words, "Your miracles are impressive, God, but I'd be a lot more comfortable if you'd send someone else to do them for Pharaoh. I'd rather watch from a distance. I'll cheer for the other guy . . . just don't send me."

Many of us say we want to know God's will for our lives, but when He begins to show us, we respond with fear and dread . . . and a sudden desire for the comfort of the sidelines. We begin to take our eyes off of God and focus instead on our own perceived shortcomings. "O Lord," said Moses, "I have never been eloquent, neither in the past, nor since you have spoken to your servant. I am slow of speech and tongue" (Exod. 4:10). But he was a tad too humble. In Acts 7:22, Stephen said of Moses, "Moses was educated in all the wisdom of the Egyptians and was *powerful in speech and action*" (emphasis added). There's no proof that Moses had a stuttering problem or a speech defect. In fact, just the opposite was said of him.

Isn't it curious how "humble" we can become when we want to nominate someone else for the job God calls us to? Moses was demonstrating the kind of exaggerated humility we employ when we'd rather just watch. We're all capable of using it—the kind that says, "Oh no, not me, I'd never be any good at that," when inside we're thinking, *My fear is stronger than my faith. Let someone else do it.* Then Moses goes even further and says to God, "Not me. Send someone else." Isaiah said, "Here am I. Send me" (Isa. 6:8). But Moses said, "There's got to be someone else, send him."

What about you? Are you a spectator or a participant? Spectators watch safely from the stands, free of any of the stains or scrapes that come from being in the game. But they never feel the thrill that participants know. For years, I had the following quote from former President Theodore Roosevelt taped to the corner of my computer monitor:

> It's not the critic who counts, not the man who points out how the strong man stumbles, or where the doer of deeds could have done them better. The credit belongs to the man who is actually in the arena, whose face is marred by dust and sweat and blood, who strives valiantly; who errs and comes short again and again; because there is not effort without error and shortcomings; but who does actually strive to do the deed; who knows the great enthusiasm, the great devotion, who spends himself in a worthy cause, who at the best knows in the end the triumph of high achievement and who at the worst, if he fails, at least he fails while daring greatly. So that his place will never be with those cold and timid souls who know neither victory or defeat.[2]

I'll bet you love God. I'll bet you want to know His will. You want to see it lived out—but you might not want to be the one who's living it. You're all for sharing the faith—you're just not comfortable sharing *your* faith. You're all for making a difference, for helping people; you just don't want to be the point person for the endeavor. So in our flesh, we create our little lists that say, "I'm willing to do this for You, God, but not that. I'm willing to go here, but not there." We have a list of countries we'll visit, ministries we'll give to, projects we'll take on and committees we'll steer. Just don't ask us to do anything that's not on our list! God asked Moses to take the lead, and Moses had exhibited leadership qualities before. But he'd gotten comfortable in the middle of nowhere, tending his father-in-law's flocks, and he wasn't shopping for a tough assignment. What about you? Are you a spectator or a participant in the will of God?

A few years back, I had the great privilege and pleasure of throwing out the first pitch at a Houston Astros baseball game. I walked out to the big league mound with a regulation ball and threw it 60 feet and 6 inches, just like the big leaguers do, to the player crouched at home plate. It was a strike. A 30-mph strike, but a strike just the same. But after I threw that first pitch, I sauntered off the mound and left the game to the professionals. I went back to my seat in the stands.

Every Sunday morning, all across America, God's people sing and pray and listen to sermons—maybe some even take notes. But by Monday morning, many have walked off the field of Christ-following and retreated back into the stands, leaving the heavy lifting to the Jesus "professionals" and "navy seals" of the faith. They've taken their seat, and they're not getting up again until next Sunday. They've heard direction from God, but they believe that whatever action He's calling for could best be done by someone else. Typically, 20 percent of the people in a church do 80 percent of the giving and volunteering. "Let someone else go," they reason. "I'll stay home and send someone else." That's what Moses wanted. He said "Send Aaron!"

I was one of those guys once. I let false humility lull me into inactivity about God's work around the world. I imagined that I could contribute in my own way, on my own terms. My heart for missions was barely beating when I agreed to go on a trip to China. But I said a simple yes, and God opened my eyes. Previously, in regard to missions, I'd been content to say, "Here's $25—send Aaron." But once I participated, I no longer wanted to be just a spectator. Now I'll just about fight you for a seat on the plane! Once I trusted God to follow His leading to China, it was easier to say yes when He opened the door for me to go to Venezuela, India, Cuba, Costa Rica, Mexico, Guatemala and England on subsequent missions trips. Now I can't get enough. I tell our missions pastor that his is the only other job in the church I'd want, so he'd better look out. One simple yes brought me from unwilling spectator to more-than-willing participant, and it has even touched my family, as my son has started going with me on trips.

Even as we step out in faith there will be stumbles. Moses didn't get everything right—and neither will we. But in God's presence he experienced His strength . . . and in His will he experienced His power. Moses told God he'd never been great at talking. God said "Moses, who made your mouth? Now get out there, and I will put the words in your mouth and show you what to do."

Sometimes we can do what Moses did and dig our heels in, refusing to let God use us and supply us with the power we need. "Please send someone else," Moses finally begged. And you know what? God did. Not *in place* of Moses, but together with Moses. "What about your brother Aaron, the Levite?" God said. "I know he can speak well. He is already on his way to meet you, and his heart will be glad when he sees you. You shall speak to him and put words in his mouth; I will help both of you speak and will teach you what to do. He will speak to the people for you, and it will be as if he were your mouth and as if you were God to him. But take this staff in your hand so you can perform miraculous signs with it" (Exod. 4:14-17).

It would be a mistake for us to believe that if we say no to God He will abandon His will. He won't. He'll get it done with us or without us. But how much better to be with Him in the doing! If I had said a hardened no to God's plan to move me from the college ministry I knew and loved to the pastorate of a big city church (something I'd never done before), then someone else would have become the pastor of Houston's First Baptist Church. The church would have gone on, not waiting on me. But, thankfully, I chose to participate in His plan by saying yes, even though I could have given all the excuses Moses used, and more.

Choose to be a participant, not a spectator. Sure, you might fail. But Michael Jordan missed more than 9,000 shots in his NBA career and lost 300 games—26 of those when his coach and teammates trusted him with the ball to take the last shot. "I've failed over and over in my life," he said. "And that is why I succeed." Abraham Lincoln saw two businesses fail and lost two legislative races before he was nominated for vice president and lost. But some folks think he made a pretty good president. Albert Einstein won the Nobel Prize at age 26—but not until after he'd failed one university entrance exam and been fired from three teaching jobs![3] As Winston Churchill wisely stated, "Success is never final; failure is never fatal; it is the courage to continue that counts."[4]

Don't stumble over the "spectator or participant" hurdle. Decide now that when God shows you even the slightest glimmer of His will, you will follow it—believing that His power and strength are more than enough to accomplish His purposes. He is calling you to participate . . . to be a part of the action and not just a fan or a spectator. Go on that mission trip. Be the one who places food in the hands of the homeless. Feel that good fear when you verbally share your faith. Say yes to His call.

Two hurdles stand in the way of doing God's will on the track of your life. But neither is insurmountable. Learn to jump them, because the race of life is a tough one. The fear of what "they" say and the temptation to take to the stands are small obstacles in light of the surpassing power and greatness of God. I don't want Him to use someone else when He was looking for me. Rich Mullins said once in an interview, "In terms of eternity, those people who did the greatest things for God were the people who weren't trying to do anything at all. They were just simply being obedient. . . . Those are the people God can use. And I want to be one of them."[5]

God wants to actively move in this world through us. Through you and me. My hand is up and I'm waving it. I'm done hiding. I'm saying, "Here I am! Pick me!" That's the true path of life. "For the eyes of the LORD range throughout the earth to strengthen those whose hearts are fully committed to him" (2 Chron. 16:9).

For Further Reflection and Discussion

1. Who are the "theys" in your life? What do their voices say? What does God say? To whom will you choose to listen?

2. In what ways has God demonstrated His power in your life in the past? Can you trust Him to do so again?

3. (Circle one.) "I was created to be a spectator/participant."

4. (Circle one.) "I'm living like a spectator/participant." Why?

5. Where is a place you could participate?

Notes

1. "Informational Social Influence," The University of Idaho Psychology Department, transcript of audio lecture. http://www.class.uidaho.edu/psyc320/lessons/lesson07/lesson7-1_transcript.htm.

2. Theodore Roosevelt, cited in Brian M. Thomsen, comp., *The Man in the Arena: Selected Writings of Theodore Roosevelt: A Reader* (New York: Forge, 2003).

3. "Bio-Sketches: Michael Jordan," MyGrowthPlan.org. http://www.mygrowthplan.org/Biographies/MichaelJordan.html.

4. Winston Churchill, quoted in Clarence Warner, *The Promises of God* (Longwood, FL: Xulon Press, 2005), p. 70.

5. "Tribute to Rich Mullins," *20 The Countdown Magazine,* radio broadcast. http://www.20thecountdownmagazine.com/exclusives.php.

7

THE PART OF GOD'S WILL NO ONE WANTS

February 28, 2006. I'll never forget that day . . . but not because it was a red-letter event for the family scrapbook. That morning, Kelly and I drove to the Texas Medical Center in a hush. The radio was on, but I don't recall the song. In fact, I couldn't have told you what it was while it played. As I drove, Kelly stared straight ahead. We had planned this journey but hoped to make the trip months later, in excited anticipation and not quiet dread. We were supposed to be carrying an overnight bag with a change of clothes and tiny "onesies"—with me coaching and encouraging: "Just breathe deeply, sweetheart." Our imagined script was not to be played out that day. Instead, we were driving toward the hospital for a procedure that would place a sad period on a pregnancy that had already ended.

Twenty-four hours earlier, at a scheduled sonogram, the technician could not detect our baby's heartbeat. The doctor's confirming "I'm sorry" became the cue for our tears. I held Kelly's hand as she lay on the table and I crouched next to her in a small plastic chair. Prayers went up and tears came down.

We didn't question why or turn to anger as a salve for our raw emotions. We just ached. The God who designed the miracle of conception had called our child home before the first hug. Somehow, it was His will. It had to be. It certainly wasn't ours. The loving God that I'd preached about for 20-plus years had wounded us. Not failed us . . . *wounded* us. That morning, we discovered a part of God's will that no one wants.

I wanted instead to welcome friends and family to the hospital maternity floor while Kelly slept in recovery. I wanted to walk them to the nursery glass to peer at the tubs of infants and point to ours. Perhaps even to gesture at a tiny wrist with an armband that read "MATTE." I'm a good storyteller, and it would have been a good story. I was willing to give God all the glory for it. Kelly and I would have been first-rate parents. We looked forward to playing with our baby on the floor and capturing happy birthday parties on video for years to come. But instead, our story was one of weeks of emotional wreckage and baby gifts to return. Tears instead of terry cloth towels. The words that came to us that day were hard ones but familiar, and in a strange way tinged with a steady joy: "The LORD gave and the LORD has taken away; may the name of the LORD be praised" (Job 1:21).

Perhaps before that day, I wasn't fully prepared to answer the question, "Is it possible for life to stink and still be God's will?" Today I can say that the answer is yes. Throw a dart at the pages of the Bible and you're likely to hit a character whose story could confirm that yes. Job. Paul. David. Peter. Look at Moses, journeying for years with less-than-faithful followers, coming close to the Promised Land but without getting in.

Struggles, setbacks and wounds are undeniable facts of life. God's people don't get passed over by hardship . . . but hard times are the part of His plan we'd almost always choose to omit if the choice were ours to make.

The hard times might be easier to understand if our pain could always be traced to our own sinful choices or those of others. But struggles can and do befall us that we have had no hand in. Nothing Kelly or I did caused our baby's heart to stop beating. Sometimes the uproar of life is a natural result of choosing sin or selfishness; but just as often it is not. So how do we handle pain or heartbreak in a way that keeps us moving forward? Even if no 1-2-3 foolproof plan exists, can we at least hope in a higher way? I think we can.

Right now, I am writing with my daughter, Valerie, in my lap, and she has decided to "help." Here is her contribution to this chapter:

kstenfaiXBUKKMlksdfl //k;l;; kkkkk;;;;;;;;;;;;;;;;; kdfjlk

In a peculiar way, her interruption to my writing is part of what I am trying to say. If we had not suffered the miscarriage, it is possible that Valerie would not be here. Obviously, conception is God's business. He is the giver of life. But in Kelly's and my little microcosm of planning, the child now in heaven—and I do believe babies go to heaven—would have completed our family.[1] We would not have tried again. Now this little blonde-haired girl sits in my lap with a fuzzy bear on her shirt and her hands on my keyboard . . . and I can't imagine life without her.

Her presence speaks to a truth we all need to grip for dear life and savor well: God is working things out in the midst of those very parts of His will *we do not want*. He is crafting, shaping and planning at a deeper level than we can see. He is looking at a line that stretches from eternity past to eternity future while we are looking through a straw at a tiny black pencil dot set on that line of life. Even more specifically, we are looking at the shavings of that dot that incorporate the last month or the next. He is looking at eons of eternity at once; we can only look at the speck of our days or months or years.

Stay Put . . . He Is in Control

When Moses and the children of Israel stood at the edge of the Red Sea, with the Egyptian army closing in, they made an almost unbelievable tactical choice: they stayed put. They stood in place. Why? Because God was weaving a story that a bridge across the water could not tell. The Israelites would have to walk *through* the sea to tell God's great story of deliverance. Surely there were other routes, other plans of escape, but "God did not lead them on the road through the Philistine country, though that was shorter" (Exod. 13:17). Certainly battles awaited them on the "shorter roads" too—but God wanted to take them the long way in a story that required an unprecedented miracle: the parting of the Red Sea.

"Our whole perspective changes," says Robert J. Morgan, in his book *Red Sea Rules*, "when, finding ourselves in a hard place, we realize the Lord has either placed us there or allowed us to be there, perhaps for reasons presently only known to

Himself."[2] His goal for the hemmed-in Israelites was not the "dot" of the moment Moses must have seen through his straw-like perspective, but a timeless story of God's greatness that would be told and retold throughout history.

When you and I begin to look at the whole of God's plan instead of the tiny part immediately before us, trust opens up. We can trust our great God to see us through. He has been faithful to those who've come before us, and He will be faithful to us. The psalmist wrote, "Your faithfulness continues through all generations; you established the earth, and it endures" (Ps. 119:90).

Martyrs, widows, orphans, the impoverished, the forgotten, the persecuted and the wounded have all found Christ faithful. With such a rich history behind Him, He is not going to ruin His reputation by hanging *us* out to dry. He doesn't just *act* faithfully; He *is* faithful. I don't just act like Gregg Matte—I am Gregg Matte. That is who I am, and all that I can be. He is faithful. That is who he is, and it is all that He can be. "The one who calls you is faithful," Paul wrote to the Thessalonian church, "and he will do it" (1 Thess. 5:24). And again, to the church at Corinth he wrote, "God, who has called you into fellowship with his Son Jesus Christ our Lord, is faithful" (1 Cor. 1:9).

Even in the most difficult times, we can trust deeply that the parts of His will we don't want are the very things He will use to accomplish His eternal plan! He is faithful not to wound us at random; He is faithful to save us forever. Throughout our lives we will surely experience pain and heartache, but they are not meant to thwart the mission of the Lord, but to further it!

So keep standing. Keep trusting. Echo Peter's words as your declaration of truth in troubled times:

> From this time on many of his disciples turned back and no longer followed him. "You do not want to leave too, do you?" Jesus asked the Twelve. Simon Peter answered him, "Lord, to whom shall we go? You have the words of eternal life. We believe and know that you are the Holy One of God" (John 6:66-69).

As Jesus drew closer to the cross and to His death, His disciples became more and more frightened and disoriented (see Matt. 26:47-56). This was not the kind of trouble they signed on for! They were hoping for something more "secure" than a persecuted Messiah marching straight into sure conflict and hinting at how He might die. Not surprisingly, some of His followers began to fall away. But Peter had it right. Although his response was just as counterintuitive as Moses' improbable "stand still" at the Red Sea, he understood that the very best thing for them at the time was to press in even closer to Jesus than before. There was no better place for them to be.

Movement doesn't always improve our situation, any more than putting on a blindfold and turning 10 circles around a piñata refines our swing! We only lose sight of our target and lose our equilibrium. Those times when we want to move somewhere—anywhere!—just to keep from feeling trapped are the very times we need to be still and lean in closer to embrace His will. Don't leave . . . cleave! It seems counterintuitive, but the more closely you walk with Christ in the uncomfortable or the unknown, the greater clarity of life you will experience. Are you confused? Hurt? Disoriented? Cling to Christ and His Word like never before.

A word to the wise: Getting mad doesn't help either. Anger is usually a secondary emotion that follows hurt or disappointment. It doesn't achieve the will of God (see Jas. 1:20). In tough times our anger and resentment can begin to simmer. When it does, we imagine that by drifting away or giving the God of the universe the cold shoulder, we can teach Him a thing or two about how to treat a friend. Our drift is our way of saying "Well, fine then, have it Your way"—and the beginning step in seeking an ally that will love us better than God. Some see alcohol as a ready friend offering quick comfort. Others believe a church switch to a place where "people really understand me" will relieve their pain. Coping mechanisms and strategies for handling hurts and disappointments abound. But regardless of the action we choose, we're focusing again on a tiny pencil dot on the line of eternity.

Maybe that very realization is what prompted Peter to declare to Jesus, "Where else would we go?" Our version might sound more like this: "Lord, chief of the universe, what could we possibly try? Mind-numbing entertainment? Self-help best-sellers? Codependency? An eating disorder? Drug or drink? Who or what besides You holds the words of eternal life?"

The trials of life are meant to push us closer to Christ. The night of Jesus' betrayal, we find John reclining at the table with his head on his Master's chest (see John 13:22-25). Imagine if, in the moment Jesus announced that one of His disciples would betray Him, John's head had been resting on Jesus' chest. Wouldn't his reflexive response likely have been to quickly lift his head and draw back in shock? Those words could have either placed a wedge between the two of them or drawn them closer together. John could have leaned in to hear more closely the heartbeat of Jesus, or pulled away. In my imagination, I see him move away, and then see Jesus place His hand gently on John's head to draw him near again.

Near Jesus is exactly where I need to be when troubling words or wounding circumstances come. This kind of intimacy can feel a little uncomfortable for some, and particularly for men. But the physical image points to a deeper spiritual reality—one my own children have helped me understand. When one of my kids wants to crawl into my lap and press in close after a skinned knee or a scary dream, I can't help but be reminded of the tender love God has for His children. I want Greyson and Valerie to be completely comfortable and secure in my arms. I am glad to be the one they run to. Think about it: There is a short list of folks who have an open invitation to place their head on your shoulder or chest. My list includes only three: Kelly, Greyson and Valerie. No one else gets those kinds of hugs, because there is a depth of relationship that precedes such intimate contact.

When I am hurting, when I'm experiencing that part of God's will that I do not want, He is the one I run to. The truth is, God has "rigged" this life to require Jesus Christ at its center: "He is before all things, and in him all things hold together" (Col. 1:17). Faced with the part of God's will I do not want, He is the One I draw close to, trusting that He is weaving a plan—even when I don't understand how.

Through that difficult morning of loss and heartbreak, Kelly and I learned immeasurable lessons in trust. We chose to pray and believe that God was in control. It is somewhat easy to write about it now. It was much harder to live then. We returned home from the hospital and cranked up some of our favorite songs of praise on the stereo . . . and we cried. We focused our attention on God and pressed in to Him, hurting, but knowing it was Him we needed most. We didn't like His will and did not want it, but He didn't ask us about that. He does not have to. He is the Sovereign One. My job is to cling to Him in trust:

> Though the fig tree does not bud and there are no grapes on the vines, though the olive crop fails and the fields produce no food, though there are no sheep in the pen and no cattle in the stalls, yet I will rejoice in the LORD, I will be joyful in God my Savior. The Sovereign LORD is my strength; he makes my feet like the feet of a deer; he enables me to go on to the heights (Hab. 3:17-19).

Shine

The morning I described at the beginning of this chapter was incredibly difficult, but unfortunately, the afternoon would prove just as challenging. Sometimes when it rains, it pours.

After our "big cry," we looked at the clock and dried our eyes, then did a five-minute "power pick up" around the house to make it presentable for the guest we were expecting within an hour or two. When the doorbell rang, we opened it to Kelly's mom, Julie, and what a welcome sight she was! I'll probably never fully understand the depth and intensity of the mother-daughter bond, but I could tell Julie's hug meant more to Kelly than words can describe. I guess a part of us never outgrows the longing to hear a parent say, "It's going to be okay." Julie was always a wonderful mother to Kelly, and a wonderful mother-in-law to me.

Unfortunately, Julie's visit was not simply to be with Kelly and me during a tough time. She was facing a challenge of her own, an equally difficult part of God's will, which she didn't want. In less than 24 hours, we would return to the Texas Medical Center for hours of testing. Ultimately, a combination of chemotherapy—the process of polluting her body with powerful chemicals that we prayed would be a friend to life while foe to her cancer—and radiation were chosen as treatment.

As I wrote earlier, my in-laws, Charles and Julie, hailed from a small Texas town that I've joked would fit into our worship center with room left over. I like to affectionately call them "kountry cookin'" (yes, with a *k*). Think of a Texas rancher and his wife living a mile down a dirt road, and you'll get the picture. Charles team ropes as a "heeler" for fun. For those of you who are not from the country, team ropers lasso a calf from horseback—one roper, the "header," going for its head and horns, and the other for its heels. We're talking top-of-the-food-chain type living here. (Animal activists had best stay put in the city.) Here men eat beef and shoot things for sport. The ladies usually prefer to stay in and keep the home fires burning. Julie used to bake two loaves of homemade bread every week—and they came out of the oven on Sunday afternoon when she returned from playing in the hand bell choir at church. Theirs is a simple way of life for good, honest people—a throwback to the pace and priorities of a generation or two ago.

Julie arrived that afternoon with luggage she probably hadn't used in a while, prepared for a stay in the fourth largest city in the U.S. and treatment at one of the top cancer centers in the world. A church member recommended to us a specialist in kidney cancer, the primary site of Julie's cancer, although it was spreading. As we sat and talked in the living room, I was struck with the strength God was displaying through my wife. She had just lost a baby and was now conversing with her dying mother with kind, tender, understanding words. And she was shining with the love of Jesus Christ.

The next months were filled with regular trips to the M.D. Anderson Cancer Center for Julie's chemo. We drove her to each appointment, because when you live on a dirt road, directions like "take I-10 east to 610 Loop South, exit at Fannin and park in TMC Garage 7" aren't very helpful. Many times I would act as "scribe," taking notes for Julie while the doctor used strings of 10-syllable words to say, "You are dying." Sometimes after these appointments we would share a meal at the hospital cafeteria or a nearby restaurant to celebrate if the news of the day was encouraging, or commiserate if it was not. Through it all, Julie shined too.

I remember one evening seeing Julie asleep in a chair at our house with her Bible in her lap. In the midst of spending time in prayer, she sweetly dozed off. I just teared up and turned out the light, feeling like I had seen firsthand the peace that only God can give. She consistently chose prayer over complaint and spiritual growth over worry. She displayed a depth of trust that had to come from pressing in close to her Savior.

More than We Could Handle

Medicine did all that medicine could do, but it could not stop the rapid growth of Julie's cancer. So she went back to her small town to wait to be called home. She was happier there, but the distance was harder on us. Instead of 10-mile drives to the Medical Center, we were making 200-mile trips to the ranch. Kelly would go back and forth, and I would keep the house in Houston running. My kitchen skills tend more toward take-out than homemade, but at least I kept a small number of restaurants in business. Words like "hospice" and "end care" became familiar to us. Parties were planned to give friends and family a chance to say good-bye. For us the hurt over the loss of a baby morphed into the pain of losing a precious mother and mother-in-law. Both were awful.

Have you ever heard someone say, "God will never give you more than you can handle"? I'm guessing they're paraphrasing 1 Corinthians 10:13, which says, "He will not let you be *tempted* beyond what you can bear" (emphasis added). But trouble and temptation are two different things. There will never be an instance when you or I are forced into sin with no way out. Sin is always a choice, not the inevitable result of crushing temptation. But somehow that verse has been twisted to mean that we won't experience more trouble than we can bear—when in fact nothing could be further from the truth. God will *often* allow more than we can handle, but He'll never allow more than He can handle. In fact, my whole life is more than I can handle—that is why I need Christ!

I needed God to stay the course while I was in school. I needed Him as a single man who longed for a spouse. I needed

Him when I needed a job. Now, with two kids, a marriage, friends and a great church to love and lead . . . I definitely have more than I can handle. I need God when Kelly and I struggle to be "two who became one" and we're arguing over which one of us we became! Only in His strength and wisdom can I know what is best for my family and whether or not my desires are selfish or pure. It is possible to "win the fight" but lose ground in marriage . . . a lesson most of us have learned the hard way. Bottom line, this life is hard. I need God every minute of every day, because I am often faced with "more than I can handle." Paul must have understood this when he wrote these words to the Corinthian church:

> We do not want you to be uninformed, brothers, about the hardships we suffered in the province of Asia. *We were under great pressure, far beyond our ability to endure,* so that we despaired even of life. Indeed, in our hearts we felt the sentence of death. *But this happened that we might not rely on ourselves but on God,* who raises the dead. He has delivered us from such a deadly peril, and he will deliver us. On him we have set our hope that he will continue to deliver us, as you help us by your prayers. Then many will give thanks on our behalf for the gracious favor granted us in the answer to the prayers of many (2 Cor. 1:8-11, emphasis added).

Great pressure results in great reliance. God will undoubtedly allow more than we can handle. Settle it and rely on Him. The "I can't do this" sweat of life is where we learn to trust Him most deeply. "Trials and troubles are dumbbells and treadmills for the soul," writes Robert Morgan. "They develop strength and stamina."[3] God has used the pressures of miscarriage and cancer to draw me closer to Him. They both looked as "uncrossable" to me as the Red Sea and Pharaoh's advancing army must have looked to Moses. But such challenges force our hand and cause us to rely on God more deeply than we might otherwise. Sadly, if we could handle these things without Him, many of us would try.

When was the last time you prayed for the strength just to take a single step? Today you can bet that someone in a hospital or a physical therapy clinic somewhere is asking God for that much strength. That single step to them looks impossible. It is more than they can bear. They need their God just to shuffle a few feet forward—and when they do, the resulting celebration will be even louder than the cheers for someone else's sub-four-hour marathon!

Those difficult times—those parts of His will that we do not want—cause the volume of our faith to get turned up. C. S. Lewis said that God "whispers to us in our pleasures . . . but shouts to us in our pains: it is his megaphone to rouse a deaf world."[4] Not only do *we* hear God more clearly, but our attentiveness to Him can also cause the ears of others to incline toward words of hope.

I never once heard Julie complain as she suffered with cancer—nor did I hear her preach. But her trusting faith preached. Volumes. She shined in her hard wilderness of struggle. And my wife did too. As Kelly endured a miscarriage and the loss of her mom, she sought God like never before. You should see her Bible. It looks like it fell into the blender! Ink stained, pages curled, writing in every margin, cover torn. But the wear of her

Bible also shows the protection of her heart. Imagine a woman losing a child, caring for her cancer-ridden mother and then speaking the eulogy at her mother's funeral. It was more than she could bear. But she trusted God to bear it for her, and He did. She leaned into Him and not away, and once again He proved Himself faithful.

When God's will is not what you wanted, you've received your chance to shine. So stay put and trust as you lean into Jesus. He will surely see you through.

> But in your hearts set apart Christ as Lord. Always be prepared to give an answer to everyone who asks you to give the reason for the hope that you have (1 Pet. 3:15).

For Further Reflection and Discussion

1. When have you experienced a part of God's will you did not want? How did you respond?
2. What does it mean to you to "stay put and lean into Christ" during tough times?
3. Have you ever seen someone "shine" in the face of great challenge or adversity?
4. How can you learn from and imitate their response?

Notes
1. In 2 Samuel 12:22-23, David said he would go to his child upon his death.
2. Robert J. Morgan, *Red Sea Rules* (Nashville, TN: Thomas Nelson, 2001), p. 7.
3. Ibid., p. 96.
4. C. S. Lewis, *The Problem of Pain* (New York: Harper Collins Publishers, 2001).

8

PINK KITCHENS AND BROWN BRICKS

A man sees a bush burning and moves in closer to investigate. A voice from heaven speaks to the man and gives him direction. Some intense Q&A ensues, and the man receives his assignment. Then the *real* fun begins.

Have you ever felt certain you understood what God was asking of you and moved ahead with enthusiasm, only to hit an unexpected brick wall or have cold water thrown on your efforts? That's often how it goes when we are discovering God's will for our lives. At some point, we're sure to be met with resistance, become confused or even be wounded in our pursuit of His plan for our life. We're going to say, "Lord, what's up with the conflict? I thought I was listening to You! Didn't *You* tell me to go this way?"

I had just graduated from college and was spending the summer speaking at youth camps. I felt that God was calling me not to a corporate career, but to some form of ministry, but I wasn't at all sure what that might look like. I did, however, have a strong impression that it might mean staying at Texas A&M

and continuing to lead Breakaway, the student Bible study I'd started as an undergraduate. At some point during that summer, I sat down with a minister and shared my dilemma: "I'm struggling," I told him. "I feel like I am supposed to go back to A&M and really dig in to this Breakaway thing. It's just that we don't have any money, and nothing really official, no office or staff, just me. Could God really be asking me to do *that*?"

"Gregg," he said, "this may be a time in your life when you could easily risk it all. You're not married, you don't have any bills to speak of, you don't have children . . . you're going back and forth to seminary in Houston, but you could still give the Breakaway thing a go and see what God might do. And if He calls you in another direction from there in a year or so, no problem."

His words made sense to me. *Yes,* I thought, *that's what I'm going to do. That's what I need to do.*

So, with the ink fresh on my diploma, I shouldered my backpack again and returned to the campus. No longer a student, on the first day of the fall semester I returned to the student center, a campus hub for gathering, eating and just hanging out between classes. In a short time a group of students began to collect, and one of them looked at me and said, "Gregg, didn't you graduate? What are you still doing here?"

Feeling a sense of embarrassment creep over me, I said, "Well, I'm here to continue doing the Bible study." He looked surprised. "You mean Breakaway? Couldn't you find a job?"

Everyone in the circle began laughing, and I'm telling you, it wounded me. The words and laughter felt like daggers in my heart. It felt like the people God had called me to serve had just turned on me. So I made some dumb joke about being overqualified for everything else, but believe me—I wasn't laughing on the inside.

When the circle broke up, I wandered over to a corner and sat down feeling totally deflated. "Lord," I asked, "was it You I heard, or not? Did I misunderstand Your plan? Why am I so embarrassed right now, and why am I so ashamed to be following You?" I thought I'd seen a burning bush—at least a glimmer of one—and now I felt like water had been poured on it, dousing the flame in an instant. I had been excited about what I thought was God's will—excited about reaching out, risking and seeing what God might do. But in the instant the water hit, I felt scared and uncertain too.

If you decide to walk with God and follow His voice, someone at some time is going to throw cold water on your burning-bush plans. The closer that person is to you and the more influential in your life, the more it is going to hurt. Often the deepest pain comes when family dowses the flame. Sometimes finding God's will makes life harder. Things can actually get worse before they get better!

In Moses' case, he received direction from God and determined to obey Him. Following the instructions he'd been given, Moses took Aaron and went before Pharaoh, demanding, "This is what the LORD, the God of Israel says: 'Let my people go, so that they may hold a festival to me in the desert'" (Exod. 5:1).

Pharaoh was the boss man of Egypt—a king who was worshiped like a god and who believed he *was* a god (at least a little-g god). He was accustomed to receiving worship, not demands. He decided what and where and when, as far as the business of

Egypt was concerned, and he surrounded himself with magicians boasting demonic powers who stood ready to do his bidding. So what do you suppose Pharaoh said when Moses and Aaron finished their bold speech? His words indicate that he was neither intimidated nor impressed: "Who is the LORD," he said, "that I should obey him and let Israel go? I do not know the LORD and I will not let Israel go" (v. 2).

Then Moses followed up his first request, in case Pharaoh didn't fully get the picture: "The God of the Hebrews has met with us. Please let us go on a three days' journey into the wilderness that we may sacrifice to the LORD our God, lest he fall upon us with pestilence or with the sword" (v. 3, *ESV*).

An 80-year-old man whose people were in slavery demanded their release from a powerful ruler who believed he was a god. Pharaoh was not buying it! Moses' bit about the three-day journey was a way of saying that the "trip" would be a formal one with lasting consequences, and that worship of the God of Israel was their goal. But Pharaoh was saying, in effect, "Why should I allow this? I don't know your Hebrew God, and so I have no compulsion to follow His commands."

Remember how we said that discovering God's will results from discovering the *God* of God's will? Pharaoh didn't know God. He did not walk in God's will because he did not know the God of Abraham, Isaac and Jacob. Moses had heard from the true God. But Pharaoh hadn't. Not yet. He didn't know it, but he was setting himself up in direct opposition to God; this was a dangerous position because, as C. S. Lewis has said, "When you argue against Him you are arguing against the very power that makes you able to argue at all."[1]

You're Part of a Bigger Story

You may know God, and believe you know God's will, but that knowledge could very well place you in opposition to those who do not share it. You have to understand in such times that you are part of a bigger story, a narrative that is still being written. Your circumstances may not immediately improve (or might even worsen) as a result of your knowing, but you are in a far better position than you might think. Why? Because knowing God is the purpose of life. Knowing His will is not our primary mission. Our primary mission is to know *the God of God's will*. Opposition might be a part of the story—but it is never the full story. There's always more.

Some time ago, my grandfather died. I've officiated at many funerals, but doing his was tough. I cried through the whole thing. I guess I should have been "more professional" but I couldn't. I told my wife afterward how strange it seemed to me that my grandparents' house that I'd known so well through holidays and visits was now empty. I knew the contours of that house, its smells and sounds. I knew the bedroom I slept in when we visited, and how we would close the door to the hallway at night so that air from the window unit air conditioner would flow into the bedrooms, but not the rest of the house. I can feel that room—its cool air and soft sheets . . . but I can't go there anymore.

I can close my eyes and see my grandmother's kitchen. Everything in it was pink. No kidding: pink stove, pink refrigerator, pink walls and counters. I would sit at that counter and could even walk underneath it standing up as a kid. In the mornings, she would make eggs, and I'd say, "Granny, Louisiana chickens must be different because these eggs are awesome—they're the best in the world." And she would laugh and say "Gregg, Louisiana chickens are just the same as Texas chickens—it's just that I've been cooking eggs for 60 years now. That's why they're so good." I couldn't begin to count the number of eggs I've eaten from a plate on that pink counter, all of them delicious.

I can still see the living room where my grandfather would lie on the couch, and we'd listen together to LSU football games on the radio. But that house is cleaned out now. Someone else is mowing the yard that my grandfather tended so carefully; and someone else is eating at that pink counter. Actually, I bet they replaced it with something more hip. It's not my grandparents' house anymore. And even though I can still see it in my mind's eye as it was . . . nothing is the same.

When I think about the two of them and that little house in Louisiana, I see from God's perspective that their lives in that place were a part of a larger story. A higher purpose exists than keeping a yard mowed and counters clean. Those are good things, but they are not the most important things. Houses hold the story of people who were a part of the story of God. Bigger than bricks and mortar are the relationships inside. When we discover the God of God's will, we begin to get God's perspective.

We see that we are moving toward a place that can never change hands or fall into disrepair or be bulldozed. We begin to discover the sweet aroma of Christ, and to dream of dwelling with Him, dining with Him, in a place where a throne sits at the center of everything, where the sky is like glass and the streets like gold. We see history in pieces. God sees it as part of a seamless whole.

When Moses and Aaron stood before Pharaoh, they felt sure of their God and of what He had told them to do. But Pharaoh quickly poured cold water on the plan—he didn't know and revere their God, so how could he possibly understand God's will for the people of Israel? He couldn't. He didn't see the big picture . . . the full story. So instead of granting their request, he made things worse for them and for the people of Israel. Here's what he told his foremen in charge of the Israelite slaves:

> You are no longer to supply the people with straw for making bricks; let them go and gather their own straw. But require them to make the same number of bricks as before; don't reduce the quota. They are lazy; that is why they are crying out "Let us sacrifice to our God." *Make the work harder for the men so that they keep working and pay no attention to lies* (Exod. 5:6-9, emphasis added).

Pharaoh even called God a liar! He didn't believe God had commanded the Israelites' release; he just thought they were lazy complainers. Then he decided that he would not only *not* let the people go, but he would also make their lives as miserable as possible in their slavery. He devised a way to make their work harder: to deny them straw but require that they continue to make bricks. In other words, to take the paper out of the copy room and demand that they keep making copies, or to tell them to type yet take away their keyboards. He made the productivity he demanded virtually impossible by taking away the very materials needed to complete the job!

It gets worse before it gets better. Can you imagine the feelings of futility such a decree must have generated? Moses went in and asked for a reprieve, but he walked out not only with a denial of his request but with an edict that would make the people's lives harder and more oppressive than they'd ever been before. Where they used to have all the clay and water and straw they needed to produce bricks, now they would have to get the straw for the bricks on their own. And they would gather it not from full fields, but from fields where the sickle had already been swung—where nothing was left in the ground but "stubble." And their production quota would remain the same.

For those seeking and following God's will, you need to know that circumstances may well get worse before they get better. Darkness may come. Discouragement too. But remember the bigger picture. Don't miss the reality that you and I are part of God's grand story. Our lives represent one tiny spot, one brief pen stroke in the pages of history . . . of *His* story. As someone once said, "Life is God's novel; let Him write it." In God's grand epic tale, our lives are significant, yes, but they are not the whole story.

Moses knew it. Pharaoh did not. He thought the God of Israel was a footnote in *his* personal story. But he was wrong. Don't be confused by hardship and think that something must be amiss if you face opposition. Jill Phillips's song "Grand Design" hints at this truth: "I feel the pain but it still doesn't change who You are; nothing I feel is outside of the reach of Your arms."[2] If we imagine that God's will includes only our own personal story, we'll never make it through hardship. But if we can see our hardship as part of His grand design, we'll take comfort in His plan and His presence. We'll make it through. It's not the pink kitchen that matters, but the conversation while eating the eggs.

God's Glory, or Your Relief?

The little book *Red Sea Rules* offers great advice for anyone wrestling with hardship and hoping to be found in the will of God. Red Sea Rule #2 says, "Be more concerned with God's glory than with your relief." What do most of us do when we go through a hard time? Our first reaction is usually to say, "Oh, God—get me out of this!" We don't like hardship, don't want it and would not sign up for it if it were an elective. But it almost never is. Pastor Charles Stanley says:

> None of us would raise our hands and volunteer to experience disappointment or sorrow. However, God does His greatest work in the hard times. This is when we need to remember that whatever drives us to God is always good for us. If life is running really well, we may not think seriously about how God views us. But if we are confronted with a deep disappointment or a resounding sorrow, we will respond by crying out to Him. When we do, a wondrous thing happens: He turns in our direction—opens His arms and draws us close.[3]

The key to getting through any struggle, opposition or difficulty is to surrender to the process and seek God's glory above all. Don't get me wrong: we can pray for deliverance. Jesus did. But if God chooses instead for us to remain in the tough place, it is actually possible for us to choose personal sacrifice for His glory. (Jesus did that too.)

Be more concerned with God's glory than with your own relief. The world says to strugglers, "You don't have to put up with that. Just quit. Make it easy on yourself." But in God's great story, much more is at stake than our personal ease and comfort: His glory is at stake. "Count it all joy," says James, "when you meet trials of various kinds, for you know that the testing of your faith produces steadfastness" (Jas. 1:2-3, *ESV*). And then, "Blessed is the man who perseveres under trial; because when he has stood the test, he will receive the crown of life that God has promised to those who love him" (Jas. 1:12).

Where Do You Turn When You Hurt?

One of the most important decisions we can make when we experience great difficulty is where to turn for help. Where do you turn when you are going through a hard time? Is there a number on your cell phone favorites that represents for you a spiritual or emotional 911? When the Israelites were burdened with making bricks with no straw, they amazingly turned to their oppressor for help. That's right. They went straight to Pharaoh—the very one whose decision was making their lives miserable! Instead of turning to God and declaring their desire to serve, they sought aid from a cruel master. Three times they referred to themselves as "your servants," meaning Pharaoh's servants, not God's. Wrong answer!

> Then the Israelite foremen went and appealed to Pharaoh: "Why have you treated *your servants* this way? *Your servants* are given no straw, yet we are told, 'Make bricks!' *Your servants* are being beaten, but the fault is with your own people" (Exod. 5:15-16, emphasis added).

When you go through difficult days . . . when cold water is tossed on your burning-bush plan . . . when you're not even sure anymore what God's will might be . . . that is the very best time to get on your knees and say, "God, I turn to You. I am *Your* servant, Lord. I give you everything I have. I want to glorify You." That's what Moses did.

Moses didn't seek Pharaoh's help. He returned to the Lord and said, "O Lord, why have you brought trouble upon this people? Is this why you sent me? Ever since I went to Pharaoh to speak your name, he has brought trouble upon this people, and you have not rescued your people at all" (Exod. 5:22-23).

Moses called God by the name El Shaddai, which means all-powerful, all-giving God. "O Lord—El Shaddai—I turn to You," he said. There is no better place for us to turn when things are tough than to our all-powerful, all-giving God. The hard times should be our cue to say, "God, You are all-powerful, and I am Your servant. I will go through the fire if You want me to. I'm here, and I'm going to stay on my knees trusting You, walking with You all the way." Peter, who also understood oppression from the government, put it like this:

> It is better, if it is God's will, to suffer for doing good than for doing evil. . . . So then, those who suffer according to God's will should commit themselves to their faithful Creator and continue to do good (1 Pet. 3:17; 4:19).

The people wrongly turned to Pharaoh; but Moses turned to God. One of my favorite books on leadership, by J. Oswald Sanders, says:

[The leader] must be one who, while welcoming the friendship and support of all who can offer it, has sufficient resources to stand alone even in the face of fierce opposition in the discharge of his responsibility. He or she must be prepared to have no one but God.[4]

That's leadership. And notice that God did not explain Himself to Moses. He didn't say, "Well, Moses, here's what I am doing, and here's the reason Pharaoh refused your request and became even tougher." No. God did not explain what He had already done—instead He told Moses what He was about to do: "Now you shall see what I will do to Pharaoh; for under compulsion he will let them go, and under compulsion he will drive them out of his land" (Exod. 6:1, *NASB*).

If Moses had gone to Pharaoh instead of to God, he would likely have heard just what the Israelites did: "You are lazy, lazy people." Pharaoh saw their desire to be free and worship their God as laziness. He equated their worth only in terms of the number of bricks they were able to produce. But God equated their worth with their desire to worship Him. He wants us to know that our desire for Him is not laziness. To the self-reliant, faith will seem lazy; but not to God.

God Is Bigger than Bricks

Every culture has a list of things that define success. Pharaoh's did, and ours does too. When we cease to see ourselves and our lives as part of the grand plan of God, and we see Him only as the facilitator of "the grand plan of me," we leave ourselves disconnected and at risk. Without His plan and His perspective, we're at the mercy of our culture, endlessly checking boxes on selfish lists of accolades. Our culture tells us that we are the sum total of our accomplishments or attractiveness.

We're all about business. The thrill of the deal emboldens our culture. A Starbucks coffee cup and a Bluetooth earpiece suggest importance: "I'm so busy that I must do 15 things at once, and I can't stop for anyone or anything." The measure of success for many an American man is how many "bricks" he can produce in a given period of time. For women, the measure of success is often sexuality. I'm not speaking against beauty here, or against fashion or caring about your appearance. I'm speaking against an alluring way of presenting oneself that says, "You want it, but you can't have it." That kind of blatant sexuality has been bolstered by the applause of our culture. I was watching a network news/talk show one evening where the death of a teenager was the topic, and this particular teen had died from complications of breast enhancement surgery. The beautiful female host, wearing a low-cut blouse, asked, "Where to do these girls get their unrealistic view of body image?" to which I wanted to say to the television screen, "From *you*, Miss Cleavage—where do you think?" Our culture worships materialism and sex because we have walked away from what truly deserves our worship: God Himself.

If I could say one thing in this chapter that you would take to heart and remember, it would be this: Men, you are more than the sum total of the bricks you can make. Accomplishment does not dictate your value. Far from it. There is a purpose to your work that supersedes earthly reward. And, women, you were made for something more than the *creation* of an alluring visual display. Your value does not stem from that. There is a gentle and quiet spirit residing in you that is the source of all true beauty (see 1 Pet. 3:3-6). Trusting God for these things does not make you lazy. Relying on Him for your worth does not make you "less than." Trust is not laziness; it's a belief in a higher purpose than brick making.

Finally, God's will requires God. After cold water is poured on the flame of Moses' burning bush when Pharaoh says, "No, I will *not* let your people go—instead I'll make their situation even more intolerable," Moses turns to the Lord. And over and over again, God reminds Moses that He *is* the Lord. He *is* God. "I am," He repeats to Moses. And "I will," He reiterates. God's will requires God. Period. Discover God and you will discover His will. Discover God's will and you'll be able to walk through whatever hardship comes . . . with Him. He is bigger and more powerful than you can imagine, and you and your struggles are a part of His story.

There's a moment in C. S. Lewis's book *Prince Caspian* (one of the Chronicles of Narnia) that beautifully illustrates this. Lucy is reunited with the great lion Aslan, the rightful king of Narnia, whom she has come to love and trust. Aslan represents Christ in the story:

> The great beast rolled over on his side so that Lucy fell half sitting and half lying between his front paws. He bent forward and touched her nose with his tongue. His warm breath came all around her and she gazed into his large, wise face.
>
> "Welcome child," he said.

"Aslan," said Lucy, "you're bigger!"

"That's just because you are older little one," he answered.

"Not because you're really bigger?"

"I'm not. But each year you grow you will find me bigger."[5]

Christian, each year you grow in Christ you will find Him bigger. Each time you endure hardship and keep looking to Him for guidance, you will find Him bigger. As our kids get older, we parents get smaller it seems. We're superheroes when they're two and three years old, and then they get to be teenagers and think they know it all. Our pink kitchens don't seem big enough to hold their curiosities. But God, as we get to know Him over time, gets bigger, not smaller. When life gets tough (and it will), and following His will gets hard (and it will), imagine yourself resting between the giant paws of a great and loving Lion, where nothing can touch you that does not first come through Him. Then imagine His breath kissing you with the sweetness of grace, and rest there. You are held by the great Lion of the tribe of Judah, Jesus Christ—and He leads you forth into His will when you run to Him.

For Further Reflection and Discussion

1. Describe a time when you lost the sense that you are a part of God's grand story.
2. Have you ever been asked "to make bricks without straw"?

3. Has following God's will ever been more painful after you've said yes?
4. To whom do you turn when life gets hard—to God, or to your own self-reliance? Why?
5. Why does God "get bigger" as we grow?

Notes

1. C. S. Lewis, *Mere Christianity* (New York: Harper Collins, 2000).
2. Jill Phillips, "Grand Design," from the *Writing on the Wall* CD (New York: Sony Music, 2003).
3. Charles Stanley, *Landmines in the Path of the Believer* (Nashville, TN: Thomas Nelson, 2007), p. 39.
4. J. Oswald Sanders, *Spiritual Leadership* (Chicago, IL: Moody Press, 1994), p. 174.
5. C .S. Lewis, *Prince Caspian* (New York: Harper Colins, 1951), p. 380.

9

LONGING WRONGLY

Get ready for a weird sentence. I'll write it first, and then explain it: I lust for retirement. Now, retirement may seem like an odd object of lust, a word we frequently associate with sex, but my thesaurus says it's an appropriate synonym for the kind of yearning desire I feel for "the golden years."

If there's any group of folks I get jealous of, it's retirees. Their accomplishments are secure, their plaques hang on the wall and their trophies sit on the shelf. No more work required. For retirees, a project around the house represents not a looming deadline, but a fun excuse to tinker. Resources are drawn each month that result from years and years of clocking in. The travel section of the newspaper offers real possibilities, not just fodder for daydreams—and a need for baby-sitting never enters into the equation. Retirees' time is their own. I know—I see them at Starbucks from time to time. I'm the one rushing in from my previous appointment with my hair on fire; they're the ones sipping on coffee and finishing that long newspaper article in one sitting.

I long for this stage of life, particularly on the difficult days . . . days when I feel like I'm trying to set up a tent in a

Chicago windstorm instead of reading a good book by a roaring fire. For me, the jury is still out on whether my life will become a cautionary tale or a hero's memoir. The retiree, on the other hand, can look back with satisfaction on a lifetime of accolades. I think of retirement the way a guy in a coach seat thinks of first class: if I could just get up there, I'd enjoy the rest of the trip!

But maybe my lust isn't so unusual. Perhaps I'm not the only one. In Mark Buchanan's wonderful book *The Rest of God*, he states:

> A typical response to threat and burden is to want to flee it. It's evacuation as the cure for trouble. "If only I could get away" is our mantra. Then I would be safe and then I would enjoy my life. But what we find is that flight becomes captivity: once we begin to flee the things that threaten and burden us, there is no end to the fleeing.[1]

I'm sure that Moses, our tour guide for nine chapters, wanted to retire at times and escape from the day-to-day troubles of his wilderness leadership assignment.

Even so, I imagine that retirees reading this book might be chuckling by now and saying, "It's not all it's cracked up to be!" I heard one retiree define the stage of life I lust for as "Waking up with nothing to do and going to bed without getting it all done." Maybe those who have completed "my" leg of the race lust for early morning meetings and memos, a house full of kids and afternoons spent carpooling. I don't know. In any case, I'm pretty sure the planned relief of daily vocational stress isn't meant just for TV watching or napping, but for the opportunity to do the more important work of serving the Lord and loving family and friends.

My point is, we often lust for someone else's life—or at least for their chapter of life . . . especially when the going in our own life gets a little tough. Retirement may seem like a silly lust, and when I look at it more deeply, it probably is. But to me it's comparable to the woman who can't wait to be married; or the married couple who can't wait to have a child; or the teenager who can't wait to get out of his parents' house and live on his own. Regardless of our age or stage of life, we've all found ourselves in that "Give me the next chapter of life" mode. If life had a fast-forward button, a lot of us would use it to reach whatever it is we deem more attractive than today's agenda. But it's one thing to long; it's another to lust.

By the same token, many people want to press the rewind button. We tune into radio stations playing our favorites of the past in efforts to escape to an easier chapter of life. Great comfort is found in mentally returning to a chapter of life we know we survived instead of venturing into an unknown future. Oddly, the Israelites lusted for the rewind button back into slavery: "If only we had died by the LORD's hand in Egypt! There we sat around pots of meat and ate all the food we wanted, but you have brought us out into this desert to starve this entire assembly to death" (Exod. 16:3). Wow, slavery was preferable to freedom! Strange decisions are made in hunger. Lust is deceptive hunger that can send you longing forward or backward.

I wonder how you would fill in the blank: "I lust for
_____." Would the word in your blank be
"ease," "appreciation," "wealth" or "influence"? What would the
"greener grass" be for you? I've confessed to you that my greener
grass of choice is ease, but every object of lust comes with a hidden
price we may not be willing to pay. Think about it. A large
inheritance very likely means the death of someone dear. A very
comfortable income may be the result of years of working 12-
to 15-hour days and the loss of close family relationships. All of
a sudden that greener grass begins to look like spray paint on
plastic turf, doesn't it? Celebrity seems enviable until we realize
the hollow satisfaction of being loved for what you do and not
for who you really are. Modern media worship Hollywood types;
but in that airbrushed bubble, marriages fail by the day, and re-
hab stints for various addictions appear as common as a cold.
Besides, living the perceived lifestyle of someone else is not why
you've been placed on planet Earth!

My friend Dwight Edwards has a great reminder for those
of us who fantasize about trading places. He says, "When you
crave someone else's life, remember you must trade for it *all*."
That means if you want their house, then you must take their
job. If their busy schedule seems invigorating, then you must
forfeit time with your wife and kids. If you want their marriage,
then you must deal with their in-laws (and "outlaws," too). If
you lust after their better vacation locations and more expen-
sive cars, you get their bills, as well. Personally, when I think of
that kind of wholesale trading, I'd rather stay in my own yard.
Thinking of "trading for it all" kills my heart of jealousy and
lust for another person's journey. If I can only get the fruit of

their life by abandoning the roots of my own, then I'd consider the trade too costly!

Originals and Counterfeits

God is a personal God, and He has created me and placed me in this life I live:

> From one man he made every nation of men, that they should inhabit the whole earth; and he determined the times set for them and the exact places where they should live. God did this so that men would seek him and perhaps reach out for him and find him, though he is not far from each one of us (Acts 17:26-27).

The one-of-a-kind details of God's work in our lives is far more worthy of our contentment than lusting for (and even getting) someone else's stuff could ever be. Satan is *not* the creator of originals, however. He is a counterfeiter to the core. If real "gold" is found in letting our unique differences spur one another to love and good deeds (see Heb. 10:24), then Satan's fool's gold causes us to discourage one another and sink into comparison or competition. I see this in my own life when the accomplishments of others make me feel like a failure; when their giftedness makes mine seem meager in comparison; or when I place them on a pedestal or try to knock them off. When this happens, I realize that I am no longer resting in God's creative activity, but trying to re-create myself to gain more self-esteem or worldly appreciation.

Maybe I need a little counseling—or maybe what I'm describing mirrors a common human experience: a failure to celebrate the different journeys we travel as we follow Christ. Just because you don't have a child doesn't mean that couples who do are targets of envy or lust. Just because you are single doesn't mean you are "less than" because you don't wear a ring on your left hand. If you don't feel beautiful, remember that beauty comes from the heart, not the face: the mirror reflects God's handiwork, not His mistake!

Each of us should seek to discover and use our spiritual gifts instead of feeling intimidated by the activation of someone else's. Leaders, get to work instead of envying another entity's resources. A bigger office and a larger staff don't define your enterprise. God desires a personal and thoroughly intimate relationship with His children, knowing us from the obvious scars on our knees to the not-so-obvious scars on our hearts. He's not like a coach in a locker room handing out identical jerseys; He is weaving garments for us that are matchless, one of a kind. You were born an original. Don't die a copy!

(Holy) Desire as a Catalyst

Retirement lust aside, desire is not a bad thing. Moses longed for freedom. Wanting something more or different if placed in the right context can be a catalyst. But the longing must stem from a motive to be all God made you to be, not from jealousy or a lack of confidence. Discontentment is something of a double-edged sword. One side wounds us while the other side propels us. The "holy" side propels us to slice through the mediocrity of life and pushes us to excel. Discontent with personal appearance or a desire for better health, for example, drives a lot of folks to the gym. Fitness centers typically see a spike in memberships every January, after the results of Christmas cookie indulging appear in the mirror or on the cholesterol test. A discontentment with losing can fan a team's desire for next year's season.

Displeasure with the status quo is also a phenomenal motivator for those seeking Christ. If you know there's more to life than what you are experiencing, then that lack of satisfaction can birth motivation. Maybe that's why you are reading this book; you are looking for a way of life that is richer than what you have tasted so far. If that's the case, I jubilantly say, "Live discontent!" But longing must be balanced with a deep satisfaction as well—a longing for more of God's will while also being satisfied with where you are at this very moment in your journey with Him. Paul says it this way in his letter to his Philippian friends:

> *Not that I have already obtained all this,* or have already been made perfect, but I press on to take hold of that for which Christ Jesus took hold of me. Brothers, I do not consider myself yet to have taken hold of it. But one thing I do: Forgetting what is behind and straining toward what is ahead, *I press on toward the goal* to win the prize for which God has called me heavenward in Christ Jesus. All of us who are *mature should take such a view of things.* And if on some point you think differently, that too God will make clear to you (Phil. 3:12-15, emphasis added).

That's using holy desire as a catalyst to the life God desires!

Hurry Up and Wait

We know that God has a plan for us that is better than any we could co-opt or copy, but we have trouble translating that into our day-to-day steps. The jealous lust after another's life or journey is rooted in two things: the challenge of waiting on God and the struggle to hear His voice.

Waiting is tough. In fact, it should be a synonym for aggravating! I have a hard time making it through a slow sentence, much less a slow-down in life. No matter how many times we hear the words that God's timing is perfect, from our perspective, He sometimes seems late. Can you recall a time when you felt that God was early on something you were waiting for? Our clock starts ticking the moment we've "placed our order" at the prayer counter or felt a need. But He does not operate according to our time frame. He is altogether separate and beyond time itself: He is the self-existent, timeless one. Having never owned a watch or hung a calendar on the wall of heaven, God operates in a way that seems deaf to the insistent ticking of our clocks.

Think about the years Moses waited in the wilderness for direction, or the years he wandered in the desert without a map or itinerary—40 years in each case! We rarely have that kind of patience once, and certainly not twice. Many of us won't live to see 80 years, much less wait that long to have that eightieth birthday bring a new calling.

God's timing is perfect, though the only way we discover that truth is through waiting. The perceived delay of the cavalry coming sands our souls to greater smoothness. For 25 years, Sarah and Abraham waited on the child God had promised would be born to them. In fact, they waited until they were the age of great-grandparents to become first-time parents! Then, to a 90-year-old woman and a 100-year-old man, God gave a child whose name means "laughter": "Sarah became pregnant and bore a son to Abraham *in his old age, at the very time God had promised* him" (Gen. 21:2, emphasis added).

The years of waiting had moved Abraham and Sarah into the retirement home, but that was the very moment that God had planned to fulfill His promise. In fact, the delay was what made the miracle miraculous! Man's perfect timing highlights the craftiness of man; God's perfect timing highlights the provision of God. Only one of those is lasting.

If you are waiting on God to provide children, a spouse or a different way to answer the "What do you do for a living?" question, don't lust after what you perceive as the next thing in life. Instead, trust and submit yourself to the Lord. Wait on Him by worshiping Him and allowing Him to grow your faith. Life has no "fast-forward" button, and no "rewind" or "pause." Just "play" and "stop." If you're still breathing, then the "play" button is pushed, and the interlude of waiting is a growth opportunity to soothe and smooth your anxious heart. Try to see it as the pause between songs, not the sign that the band has been dismissed.

I know that waiting sounds extremely passive. You might equate it to sitting instead of running, when actually it is running a different kind of race—and maybe a tougher one. The sprint of activity becomes a marathon of patience as God moves your focus from the exterior of your life to the interior. If that's what is happening in your life right now, He isn't holding out on you. He is working in you, in a place no one sees.

During each leg of our journey, God is cultivating depth and maturity in us. When we wait, we trust. Control is relinquished, and faith is given in its place: "I wait for the LORD, my soul waits, and in His word I put my hope. My soul waits for the LORD more than the watchmen wait for the morning" (Ps. 130:5-6).

Waiting to Hear

Each chapter of life, from our perspective, has its delays; hopefully, as we wait, we learn to listen for the Lord's leading. When we do this, delays can become productive times in our spiritual development. When we stop asserting our nine suggestions to the Lord of the Ten Commandments, good things happen. We're restless waiters, wanting someone else's life. But blow the horns: Jesus is about to walk into the stalled and searching heart: "The LORD is good to those whose hope is in him, to the one who seeks him; it is good to wait quietly for the salvation of the LORD" (Lam. 3:25-26).

A big difference exists between *wanting* to hear from God and *needing* to hear from God. Wanting to hear from Him is great but may still mean we're keeping our own bushes burning as we look for confirmation of our own plans. Needing to hear from Him yields those "Here I am" moments when we're not pushing our own agenda, but seeking His. An empty-handed believer with a listening ear trumps a well-resourced, driven, on-the-move believer any day. The first needs to hear from God; the latter merely thinks it would be "nice" to hear what God has to say. To one, God's directive voice is an absolute necessity; to the other, it is only icing on the cake. Nice, but not necessary. Desirable, but not desperately needed.

Rest assured that each of us vacillates between needing and wanting to hear from God; but acknowledging the difference helps straighten the path. "He who has ears let him hear" is a frequent refrain of Jesus'. The Savior's intent is not to evoke emotional response from hearers, but to heighten their attentiveness to the voice of God. Emotional responses don't usually last, but the disciplined development of a "spiritual ear" will pay dividends forever.

Only through the development of a finely tuned "spiritual ear" will we be able to identify "longing wrongly." If we bounce through life impatient and indifferent to God, our lives will only be an imitation of someone else's. Living a superficial copy-cat existence searching for the fast-forward and rewind buttons is not God's will for anyone. If God wanted me to be retired, I would be in my seventies, not in my forties. I'm blessed to be in the throes of raising kids and working. The bottom line is yearning to genuinely know that God shapes your life into a treasure, not a counterfeit.

For Further Reflection and Discussion

1. What do you lust for?
2. In what ways are you tempted to trade your life for someone else's?
3. How does the idea that "you trade it all" help you to "stay in your own yard"?
4. What are the challenges and blessings that come with "waiting on the Lord"?

Note
1. Mark Buchanan, *The Rest of God* (Nashville, TN: Thomas Nelson, 2006), p. 17.

10

BIG EARS ARE BEAUTIFUL

The *Guinness Book of World Records* is filled with wacky, interesting and sometimes just gross oddities from around the globe. Records exist for things we didn't even realize people were measuring. For example, you have probably never heard of a pet rabbit named Nipper's Geronimo, right? For you animal lovers, this rabbit from Bakersfield, California, holds an interesting title in the world of rabbitry. Rabbits are widely known for big ears, but Nipper's Geronimo has the longest. His title was secured at the American Rabbit Breeders Association National Show in Wichita, Kansas, with a complete span of 31.125 inches. So imagine holding each ear out for a horizontal span of almost a yard from tip to tip.[1]

We definitely aren't after increasing the size of our physical ears, but we do desire an increase in the hearing of our spiritual ones. The Lord is speaking all of the time to us, but are we listening? Do we recognize His guiding voice and understand how He speaks? Big ears to the voice of God are a beautiful thing.

Three Ways God Speaks

God desires to speak to us in primarily three ways: through His Word, His Spirit and His people. This may sound obvious, but believing it matters. If you don't believe He wants to speak to you, you won't be quick to tune your ears to heaven. God wants to speak more than you or I want to listen. Our desire to hear Him pales in comparison to His desire to speak to us. The efforts He has already made to be heard far outweigh the half-hearted efforts we make to listen. We pray while we drive, listening to the radio and changing lanes. (We're multitaskers.) But He's focused. The Bible that bears His words to us is painted in martyrs' blood, protected by vast study and proven by transformed lives. His book is the primary mode of hearing available to us, and those who know God's Word the best hear God's voice the most. Hear that one more time, as it is tremendously important: Those who know God's Word the best hear God's voice the most.

With all of its mystery and difficult passages, the Bible is the mouthpiece of God, with a direct line to our hearts. He speaks through His Word. His Spirit wields its thin pages as a sword, determining our motives and our mindset. Sometimes a verse or two will literally pop off the page to me, like the unfolding shapes of a children's pop-up book. Countless times I have read a Bible passage and thought, *Has this always been here? It seems like it just arrived today.* This happens because the Bible is unlike any other book. It is "living and active" (Heb. 4:12), cutting through the surface chatter and going straight for the core of my heart. Its pages show me the depths of God's love and truth from history past to eternity future.

The more that God's Word gets into us, the more we will desire to get into the movement of God. How goes your time in God's Word? Is it good? Then don't become self-satisfied and let pride seep into your heart. Not so good? Then change that today.

I hope people of vastly different levels of spiritual understanding are reading this book. As I write, I have tried to keep in mind friends who are strong in their faith and other friends who are just beginning their walk with the Lord. We all want to know God's desires for us, and the Bible offers us the clearest way to do so. I have to warn you, though: His book is habit-forming. As one unknown writer has stated, "Regular use can cause loss of anxiety, decreased appetite for lying, cheating, stealing and hating. Side effects can include increased sensations of love, joy, peace and compassion."[2]

If you are just beginning to explore the Bible, a few starting tips may be helpful:

- Pick a consistent place and time to read your Bible each day.
- Begin with a short book of the New Testament (I suggest Ephesians or Philippians) in a version you can easily understand (I use the *New International Version*).
- Read a chapter each day, working through an entire book of the Bible.
- When you finish reading a book, write the date next to that book in your Bible's table of contents and feel the victory!
- Repeat these steps for life.

For those who have been at it for a while:

- Mix it up to keep things fresh. What books of the Bible have you not read? How's your Old Testament knowledge? We can lock into our own system and favorites and lock down our hearts in the process.
- Go outside to read now and then. Just sit and listen for a few moments after you read. Journal your thoughts about the passage and how you can apply it.
- Read a good bit more or less than you usually do. If you read a lot in one sitting, then ponder a verse or two. If you usually grab a verse or two on the run, sit down and read through a few chapters in a row.
- Buy a new Bible in a different version to hear the same truths put in a different way.

Reading through the Bible doesn't take as much time as you might think. To read through the entire Bible takes the average reader 70 hours: the Old Testament takes 52 hours and the New Testament, 18 hours. Tackling the book a piece at a time is doable for anyone. Make it your aim to read the Bible all the way through in the next year or two, and you will hear God like never before. It takes a whole Bible to make a whole Christian.

I look at my Bible as the workbook of my life. I write thoughts in its margins, and every person I personally baptize autographs the inside cover. In it I also write the person's name of every funeral I am asked to preach; I highlight its verses; and (don't let this get around) I write down all of the Lord's Supper references on the title page so that I'll always have them ready on the platform. My Bible is not like any other book in my library, because I don't own the Bible; it owns me.

I have another special tradition related to my Bible: I retire my old ones. Every five years or so I get a new Bible and place the old one on a shelf. Like a favorite pair of jeans, the once-crisp leather of the cover finally becomes faded and worn. The pages are filled with notes and names, and with lessons I've been taught and have taught others. My plan one day is to have at least 10 life-worn Bibles on my shelf that I can eventually give to each of my children and grandchildren. I look forward to the moments when I can place a Bible that guided my life for a season into their hands. My hope, of course, is that those tattered Bibles will preach to them a wordless sermon on the importance of wearing out their own Bibles.

A worn Bible speaks of a protected heart. Does your Bible speak to the next generation as a paperweight, or as a map of the soul? Retiring my Bible also challenges me to really know its content. My ability to find and remember verses can't be based on the aided recall of highlighted words or dog-eared pages or a star in the left-hand margin. John Calvin said, "The eyes of God will always be attentive to guard those who shall be attentive to His instructions."

Again: Those who know God's Word the best hear God's voice the most.

Listen to the Spirit

God also speaks through His Spirit. When a person trusts Christ as Savior, a radical change takes place. It is more than the elevating of his or her Friday night vocabulary and Sunday morning activity; it is the fact that the Holy Spirit takes up residence in the believer's heart. God's Spirit, the third member of the Trinity, comes to reside inside every believer. Jesus referred to the Holy Spirit as the *paraclete*, which means "one who walks alongside of." The Holy Spirit indwells Christians like a constant companion who walks alongside. He guides the thoughts and actions of believers in the way that God desires. Like a homing signal, the Holy Spirit is always directing us to God. The challenge is to tune our spiritual ears to the voice of this living guide.

"How do I know the difference between the guidance of the Holy Spirit and my own emotions?" someone might ask. I have good news here: Grounding ourselves in the Bible can help us discern between our emotions and the leading of the Holy Spirit. Emotions come and go, but God's Word remains the same. God can use our emotions to direct us, and He does, but the Spirit's guidance is consistent and deep. Here's how I would define it: The Holy Spirit's directing is a sustained movement of the heart that points to honoring God.

Notice that I said "sustained movement" and not a whim or passing fancy. Cement begins wet, but it quickly becomes solid. Our emotions vary from day to day or hour to hour, but the Holy Spirit's leading is consistent and persistent. It is sustained over time. One writer calls this leading a "sacred echo" that is heard over and over again.[3] Say for example that you have a decision to make that is basically a choice between two paths, A and B. Ask God to speak to you by laying one path heavily on your heart. As you pray, seek Him and consult His Word, one of these paths will likely become a sustained "note" in your heart;

a bush that won't burn up. I've done this with many decisions, and frequently a certain thought just won't leave me alone. Doors may begin to open as you begin to sense deeply that this is the right path for you to take.

This method does not guarantee that you will "hit the bull's-eye" of God's will 100 percent of the time. Relax in knowing that earnest attempts to follow Him—even if marked by stumbles—will go a long way to keep you on the right path.

We often imagine that our mistakes are like a trap door that drops us out of God's presence, preventing us from ever finding His will. God is not like that. Yes, our willful disobedience can take us off course, but honest seeking (even with stumbles) allows us to gracefully get up and keep walking.

Listen with your soul for the sustained voice of God's Spirit instead of listening to the crowd or to your own emotions. Remember, God wants to direct your life. Heaven does speak to humanity, and the Holy One deals with individual hearts. Hearing from God is a privilege reserved for His children, and it is part of the blessing of knowing and belonging to Him:

But the Counselor, the Holy Spirit, whom the Father will send in my name, will teach you all things and will remind you of everything I have said to you. Peace I leave with you; my peace I give you. I do not give to you as the world gives. Do not let your hearts be troubled and do not be afraid (John 14:26-27).

Be reassured that the Word of God and the Spirit of God will always combine to honor God. They will not contradict one another. If you ever sense a directing in your heart that dishonors God or is contrary to His Word, toss it out the window! The Holy Spirit and the Word of God together lead to the discovery of God's will. With these two resources, you will be deeply grounded in truth. When a "sustained movement in the heart" points you to something that honors God, trust it. Over time, the Spirit's still, small whisper will become more and more familiar to you, and you will become more adept at hearing (and heeding) it.

If you are wondering how this works, here is an example from my own life. I love to give. Kelly and I have tithed, giving at least a tenth of our income, for decades now. The sustained voice of the Spirit and the teaching of the Bible have combined to show us that our money is not really ours, but His; and even more so, the fruits of it. By settling that month-to-month facet of our finances, we are freed up to give in other ways too. Often my heart or hers will sense the wonderful Counselor advising us to give to other ministries and causes. These promptings are discernable, sustained movements of His Spirit, not dependent upon our emotions.

As I began writing this book, I felt the Spirit prodding me to give a portion of any royalties it may produce to another ministry. The prompting would not leave, and I did not want it to. I shared this with Kelly, and we began to pray. As we did, T Bar M Camps kept coming to mind.[4] This nondenominational Christian sports camp was influential in my wife's college years as she served as a counselor there; and now my kids, nieces and nephews attend each summer.

I made a phone call to the camp's director, Johnny Polk, to investigate how my gift could be used to help T Bar M's camp for kids in Peru. The kids along the Amazon River don't have access to the blessing of Christian retreat centers and the kind of camps that we do. So, T Bar M is building a camp and training Peruvians to run Camp Amazon, which is ministering to kids through an exciting, encouraging and enthusiastic camp experience. There's more info about Camp Amazon at the back of this book. Since we love camp and we love missions, it seemed like a perfect fit.

Johnny teared up on the phone as we spoke, telling me that at that moment, Camp Amazon was meeting—its campers probably lining up to go to dinner. We were both overwhelmed with the timing and plan of God. I hope that as they meet next year that dinner might be paid for by you and me. I wrote the book and you bought it. So we are members of a mission team to bless kids in South America we won't meet until heaven—what a blessing for us all!

See how it works? The foundation of giving has been laid biblically with our tithe; I sensed a leading for more, so I leaned in to listen; the leading persisted, so I made a phone call. The timing of the call coincided with the ringing of a dinner bell thousands of miles away, and the whole thing was about honoring God's name and loving His people. That sure sounds like God's voice to me—doesn't it to you?

Listen to Others

When God desires to speak, He speaks; and He has no problem delivering His message—whether through the mouths of donkeys or the mouths of men. One of the primary roles of Moses and Aaron was to declare the will of God to others, including to Pharaoh. Look at just a few of the times they were used as God's mouthpiece:

- Exodus 3:15: "God also said to Moses, 'Say to the Israelites . . .'"
- Exodus 3:18: "[Moses], go to the king of Egypt and say to him . . ."
- Exodus 4:22: "Then say to Pharaoh, 'This is what the LORD says . . .'"
- Exodus 4:28: "Then Moses told Aaron everything the LORD had sent him to say . . ."

The Lord uses His people to declare His will to His people. From the Ten Commandments to the pep talks for grumbling followers in the wilderness, God uses people to carry His word, and I'm so glad He does. That truth encourages me to turn to friends for wise counsel as well.

When I began serving Houston's First Baptist Church, I assembled a "wisdom team" of men who loved me and had no other interest in the church beyond their friendship with me. They came from all walks of life: my former youth minister, a missionary, a pastor and a jeweler. Each week I would call one of them to talk and listen for 30 minutes or so. They would each encourage me, ask me the tough questions and act as a sounding board if I needed them to.

All of us need people in our lives who love us and desire God's best for us. A friend who is neither jealous of your success nor secretly glad for your failures but wants only to see God at work in your life is a true friend indeed. We need those kinds of folks in our corner—those who are filled with the wisdom gained from their own close walk with Christ. We need the wisdom from heaven to speak through our friends, not just the help of their own opinion or experience.

One summer long ago, I worked as an intern in a student ministry. I had been wrestling with God's call to vocational ministry. During this time, I sat in church, listening to a song during the Sunday evening service in the standard "male prayer position": elbows on knees, and hands clasped to the forehead. (Not to be confused with the "I'm sleeping but want to appear to be praying posture" of elbows on knees with cheekbones resting on palms.) As I prayed that night for direction, a sweet mom of one of the high school kids left her pew and walked to mine. She touched my shoulder, and when I looked up, she politely said, "Gregg, I don't usually do things like this, but I feel like the Lord wants me to tell you that you are on the right track." I must have mumbled "thanks," and she sat down, leaving me stunned at what I had heard. I am too often shocked when I realize that God really is listening to my prayers!

God speaks through the wise counsel of good friends, teachers, pastors and even writers. He can use someone to say or write a sentence or phrase that pricks our heart and causes us to change. That's why it is so important to surround yourself with people who also desire God's will. The pack we run with matters. George Washington said, " 'Tis better to be alone than in bad company."[5] And it's even better to be in good company than to be alone. Hearing God's voice through human lips can change church from a check-the-box obligation to a burning-bush experience if we come expectantly and listen with discernment.

Discernment is essential, of course. Not every person who claims to be speaking the truth of God actually is. Keep the wisdom team in your life nearby as you listen discerningly to other voices. One evening, I was invited by some friends to hear a speaker at a church I was unfamiliar with. The "words of prophecy" were shooting out like bullets, and before I knew it, the speaker had honed in on me. *Dear God, no!* was my prayer, but it was too late: he was focused like a laser on me, and on the T-shirt I was wearing. "You in the T-shirt," he said, pointing to me. "What does it say?" He read as I showed the Reebok slogan put into "Christianese." It said, "Life is short, pray hard." (Hey, it was the 90s.)

"I like that," the speaker said. "You've been good at sports your whole life. But something has been holding you back. Right now you are being healed in the power of Jesus."

I'm sure the friends I played pick-up basketball with were hoping he was right, but they still weren't picking me first for their teams. And they shouldn't have. Nothing had changed. I had no ailment, to my knowledge, that was mysteriously healed. By all means, I believe that God can deliver specific words from the pulpit and He still heals people. But in this case, I think the speaker pieced together the message from my T-shirt and became convinced that he had a word for me from God. Be careful that the guidance you receive from others truly is from God. Don't blindly accept everything that comes your way along with a claim that it comes from Him.

Get the Garden Right

Even with the clarity of hearing the Lord's leading through His Word, Spirit and people, we can become fearful of making the wrong decision. Truthfully, we need to calm down instead of tense up. If we look back to the beginning of human history in the Garden of Eden, we find an interesting glimpse of God's will. At this time all is well, perfection on earth exists and cancer doesn't. What a great thought! One day it will literally be heaven on earth again when Christ returns. But before we look forward, we have to look backward. In the Garden, God does something that we have not thought deeply about.

> The LORD God took the man and put him in the Garden of Eden to work it and take care of it. And the LORD God commanded the man, "You are free to eat from *any tree* in the garden; but you must not eat from *the tree* of the knowledge of good and evil, for when you eat of it you will surely die" (Gen. 2:15-17, emphasis added).

God tells Adam and Eve to eat from any tree in the Garden except one. They have free rein to feast on all but one tree. God's will for the first couple was to choose from numerous good things but stay away from the forbidden one. Good trees as far as the eye can see, and one prohibited. Just one, and it is even identified for them. No tricks or deception; the trees are not squares on a cosmic minesweeper game, waiting to blow up. A right choice will not unknowingly become wrong.

Instead of breathing a sigh of relief over the tremendously good choices that outweigh the one bad choice, we reverse the garden. Unintentionally, maybe even with a heart of extreme focus, we have created a garden with one good tree and innumerable bad ones. With this perspective, seeking God's will becomes an anxious search for the needle in the haystack. We have made the hay the sin and the needle His plan.

With this way of thinking, jealousy can form when we hear a friend yell, "Found it!" in regards to God's will, causing us to either search harder or give up in discouragement. How could they have found it when we didn't? Why did they get the raise, the spouse, the baby, the attention or award instead of us? But God's will is not intended to be illusive or hidden. It is not just for a few people to discover. When someone else finds His plan, it doesn't make it harder for us. We act like there are only 10 boxes of God's will on the shelf and with every purchase by someone else we are at greater risk of an empty shopping cart.

His will isn't one hidden tree; it is a woodland. We can celebrate the job promotion or new chapter of life of a friend. A single can enjoy the kids and marriage of someone else without a "Why not me?" The blessings of another can bring a "Good for you" instead of a "Where's mine?" The trees are bountiful; each blessing of another is not "Timbeeeeer!" for your life.

I played a joke on some friends that exemplifies this type of jealousy. Years ago, Kelly and I purchased our first house and would drive friends by to see it before the closing of the sale. I bet we drove by every day like stalkers due to the excitement of buying our first home together. Sometimes we would drive by twice a day. I'm a prankster at heart, so I decided to play a little joke on our friends. Every neighborhood we have lived in has really big houses, and then our size houses. So as we pulled into our new neighborhood, I began my prankster spiel. "The house is a little bigger than we need, but we got a good deal on it." Combined with "We will have to buy a lot of furniture to fill this *casa*, but we just couldn't pass it up. The price was too good to be true."

With perfect timing, I would pull up to a different house with a SOLD sign in the yard and stop the car. As our friends looked out of the backseat window at this minor mansion, all but one said something to the affect of "It must be nice" or "That's not fair." Only one gave us an "I'm happy for you" response, and they were politely lying. My point is not that I have bad friends; I have incredible friends, but they are human. Human nature spins the Garden into a game of acquiring trees and fearing there might not be enough for me.

Thankfully, the truth of the Garden and life in relation to finding His will is that there are numerous trees to dine from. Or, said another way, the hay is His will and sin is the needle. Hunting for God's will opens up possibilities instead of closing them down. There are lots of jobs to shine the light for Christ. Don't stress on whether it is in Guatemala or Guam; just pick a country and go on a mission trip and share your faith with . . . anybody! The stress of getting everything right gives way to the freedom of the Lord. The bottom line is to walk with God faithfully in His Scriptures and by His Spirit and to be encouraged by His people. Then He will identify the tree to be avoided and the trees to gorge yourself on.

The motives of our heart can create the difference in trees. The same event can be a bad or good tree depending on the intention. One person chooses a vocation to glorify God while another just wants to get rich. One parent encourages sports to build character while another is living a vicarious dream through their kids. The same job or sport but different aims can make the difference. If you prayerfully check your motives before climbing the tree, it can save you a world of problems and pain.

As you eat heartily on the things of God, His plan unfolds. When you grasp this concept, you will look back in amazement at how He led you to the exact tree you needed. I'm married to the perfect person for me, because I decided I would only date someone who loved the Lord. The forest was godly dating in general, and He led me to Kelly in specific. I realized that glorifying God vocationally trumped a paycheck's digits; now, years later, I am amazed at the connection of my gifts and passions to my job. It is the perfect, particular tree for me. Embracing that I am to put others before myself leads to the base of trees daily that are divine appointments. Putting my heart around the forest of His will begins the journey to the individual trees. Looking back at the intricacies of His guidance acts as a catalyst to increase my faith for the future.

Moses encountered the burning bush and realized that no longer were God's people going to dine on Pharaoh's fruit. The trees of the Lord were in the Promised Land, not Egypt. God's will is the freedom of the forest, so Moses led the people from scrawny trees of slavery with poisoned fruit to a place of God's blessing.

Have you reversed the garden in your thinking? Do you think that God's will is one tree in the forest instead of the forest? If so, you probably suffer from "paralysis from analysis." You are so fearful that you will make a wrong turn that you don't even press the gas pedal. Relax; He has put the odds in your favor for following His will. Stay away from sin and run to Him, then your spiritual eyes will open to tree after tree after tree of His will. There are thousands of ways to make your life count, hundreds of ways to grow in Christ, numerous books and songs to encourage you and 66 books in the Bible to read. Just pick a place to sign up, serve, lead or read . . . pick a tree and eat and you'll be taking another step in the right direction.

For Further Reflection and Discussion

1. God speaks through His Word, His Spirit and His people. Which of these do you find easiest to hear? Which is the most difficult to hear?
2. Who do you know with "big ears" for God's voice? How does that impact their life? Are you envious of that connection?
3. How does developing an ear for God's direction keep us on the right path?
4. How does understanding the trees of the Garden bring us freedom instead of fear?
5. Right now, choose one way to increase your hearing of God's voice over the next 24 hours; reading the Bible, prayerfully listening to His Spirit or seeking wise counsel. Which will you do?

Notes
1. "Longest Ears on a Rabbit," Nipper's Geronimo, Guinness World Records, November 1, 2003. http://www.guinnessworldrecords.com/records/natural_world/animal_ex tremes/longest_ears_on_a_rabbit.aspx.

2. Cited in P. L. Tan, *Encyclopedia of 7700 Illustrations: A Treasury of Illustrations, Anecdotes, Facts and Quotations for Pastors, Teachers and Christian Workers* (Garland, TX: Bible Communications, 1996).

3. Margaret Feinberg, *Sacred Echoes* (Grand Rapids, MI: Zondervan, 2008).

4. See www.tbarmcamps.org.

5. George Washington, quoted in Tan, *Encyclopedia of 7700 Illustrations*.

11

Everyone Is Leading Someone

"Are you a leader?" A young woman working on her college application hesitated as she read the question. She felt she should say yes to increase her chances of being admitted, but decided to answer honestly and wrote no instead. Expecting the worst, she received this surprising reply from the admissions office: "Dear Applicant: A study of the application forms reveals that this year our college will have 1,452 new leaders. We are accepting you because we feel it is imperative that they have at least one follower."[1]

Almost everyone, it seems, wants to be a leader. And the truth is, everyone is leading someone.

For those who lead—either at home, in the marketplace, in a church or in a community or social organization—knowing God's will goes far beyond the personal. Leaders have followers; as the leader goes, so go the followers. If you are a leader in any arena, someone is always looking to you for direction. This is a challenge I face daily. Meetings about difficult issues or new directions regarding our church inevitably end with heads swiveling to the end of the table and someone asking, "Pastor, what do *you* think we should do?" As a leader, I expect and welcome those moments, but I also understand the weighty responsibility that goes with them.

The Tent of Meeting

Moses could relate to being in the hot seat at the end of the table. When God called him to lead His people out of Egypt, he accepted a position of influence, not affluence. Although he was being asked to lead a large number of people, Moses realized he also must be a follower himself—a follower of God. To do that, he had to spend time in the presence of God. You and I might set aside time each day to come into God's presence with our Bible, a pen, a journal and a cup of good coffee. But Moses' routine was a little different:

> Now Moses used to take a tent and pitch it outside the camp some distance away, calling it the "tent of meeting." Anyone inquiring of the LORD would go to the tent of meeting outside the camp. And whenever Moses went out to the tent, all the people rose and stood at the entrances to their tents, watching Moses until he entered the tent. As Moses went into the tent, the pillar of cloud would come down and stay at the entrance, while the LORD spoke with Moses (Exod. 33:7-9).

All the people of Israel trusted that Moses would emerge from the tent of meeting with a plan—preferably a plan that translated into practical direction and literal map coordinates. That is the epitome of looking to the leader's end of the table for direction. They stood as he passed, then saw a pillar of cloud guard the door. I don't think anyone reading this book is in quite the same position as our sandaled staff-carrier Moses, or has a comparable number of dependent followers. Facebook friends or Twitter "followers" are not the equivalent. Regardless, we all lead someone, somewhere, and we need God's leading to do our part well. The path behind us is dusty with the feet of others—so we'd better have real, reliable, burning-bush direction as our guide. Moses did not want to take a wrong turn and wind up in a cul-de-sac, saying, "Oops, wrong way," resulting in years and miles of backtracking. Neither do those of us who lead today.

Leading others can fire you up and wear you out—all in the same week. Leaders must lead, but we don't always have the complete picture. We must do what Moses did: retreat regularly to the "tent of meeting" and plead with the Lord for the next step, and the next. When I arrived at Houston's First Baptist Church as pastor, I was often asked, "What is your vision for our church?" Great question, but I lacked the big picture answer—apart from the foundational basics of shepherding the saints and teaching the Word of God. In those first days and weeks, I was doing all I could to remember staff names and find the bathroom. In fact, one day I actually got lost going to a meeting . . . in the church!

In retrospect, I am grateful that I didn't have (or give) an unstudied answer to the vision question. My lack of understanding forced assessment instead of action. A quote I clung to during that time was "Vision is understanding the past and the present in order to lead a group into the future." I don't know who first said this, but I am grateful for those words. I'm sure that other good definitions of "vision" exist, but this was the one I needed. I've been told that every church with a new pastor is in "culture shock" for the first year and should not make any major changes quickly. That sounded good to me, because I didn't know what changes to make. I had not yet assessed where we'd been and where we presently were.

Taking Inventory: Assess Your Present Situation

How can you lead anyone from point A to point B unless you know the coordinates of point A? In leading a group toward God's will, you must first know where you are. Take a clear look at your family, organization, church or other group. A strong, truthful assessment of the present is crucial to leading them into the future. For example, consider the questions I've listed here. Think of them in context of your family, vocation or ministry. Actually jot down your answers.

- What are we doing well?
- What aspects of our history have been homeruns?
- What are our fears?
- What is my deepest prayer for my family or organization?
- What short-term wins could build credibility and confidence?
- What does the preferable future look like?

As I sought to become a student of our church's history, I became restless at times for God to quickly give me the vision for our future. People (including me) were asking for direction, and heaven seemed too quiet. As God often does, He provided help in the way of wise counsel. Dennis Perry, the student minister who led me to Christ and who is one member of my wisdom team, spoke a timely word to me just as my diligent seeking was beginning to drift into discouragement. "Wait on God to bring the vision," he instructed. His calm, tender words spoken through the phone lines were just what I needed to hear. "It will come," he said.

Direction is discovered in His presence. Like Moses, leaders need time in the tent of meeting. Instead of allowing the pressure of decision making to drive a leader toward doubt or discouragement, that pressure should drive him or her to a place of seeking and trust in God. We see in the life of Moses the place we all long for: the tent of meeting where God is present, His guidance is available and His instruction is clear. When Moses emerged from the tent after each meeting, his face shone so brightly with the glory of God that the Israelites were amazed, and even a little frightened. They watched as their leader went into the tent to meet with God, and watched as he emerged from each encounter:

> Whenever the people saw the pillar of cloud standing at the entrance to the tent, they all stood and worshiped, each at the entrance to his tent. The LORD would speak to Moses face to face, as a man speaks with his friend. Then Moses would return to the camp, but his young

aide Joshua son of Nun did not leave the tent (Exod. 33:10-11).

Leaders who spend time with God are great leaders. Parents are better parents and friends are better friends as a result of spending time with God. For those of us who are married with children, our spouses and kids are depending upon us to help them navigate the difficult waters of life every day. They are asking questions of us, pushing our buttons, seeking our help—and we must respond from a resource deeper than our own strength or wisdom. We need God to lead us, so that we can effectively lead them. Notice that Joshua, the next generation of leader, was camped out at the tent of meeting, observing and learning. The leadership was trickling down and positioning the future.

This "tent time" is not about showing off or trying to look godly. It's about seeking what is an absolute necessity for every leader of any kind. As simply as I can state it: If you don't spend time consistently with the Lord, you are not going to grow. And if you are not going to grow, you are not going to know what you, your family, your church or your organization needs most. Those prioritized times alone in the presence of God should be the deep source from which you lead. Each one-on-one encounter with Him is your own personal tent of meeting. You need it—and those you lead need you to have it! They need to know that you are not simply leading from the latest self-help best-seller or your own personal opinions, but from a higher Source of wisdom and strength. Otherwise, when push comes to shove, your followers may abandon your opinions or whims, and follow their own instead. One thing is sure: If we lead by guesses and not by divine guidance, chaos will ultimately rule.

Bit by Bit

Guidance comes to the leader who spends one-on-one time with God—but it seldom comes all at once. New challenges arise daily, so guidance is required daily as well. God gave Moses signs to lead His people, but they weren't once-for-all signs; they were daily guideposts. A cloud led the Israelites on their wilderness journey by day, and a pillar of fire by night. They received manna each day—new food that miraculously appeared every morning, lying on the ground, just waiting to be collected. God often shows His will to His leaders bit by bit . . . in breadcrumbs. Knowing the destination God has in mind gives the leader and His followers greater security, but every step on the path is seldom clear.

We want it all at once, but God wants to reveal His will step by step in subsequent times of meeting. We are told He spoke with Moses as with a friend. The beauty of the New Testament is that as a result of our salvation and new life in Christ, we are His friends as well. Consider the words of Jesus:

> Greater love has no one than this, that he lay down his life for his friends. You are my friends if you do what I command. I no longer call you servants, because a servant does not know his master's business. Instead, I have called you friends, for everything that I learned from my Father I have made known to you (John 15:13-15).

Jesus calls us friends and desires to guide us as we follow Him. Can you see the trail He is marking for you? Are you following Him, or leading from your own "best guesses"? Spend time today with God. Convene with Him in your own tent of meeting, and seek to hear His voice. Live differently and seek God daily for yourself. Ask Him the tough questions. Look to Him for answers. The direction you desire will come as you seek Him. Your family and followers will be grateful for your efforts.

Because I believe this so strongly, I try to put it into practice. The first Thursday of each month I fast and pray at the retreat center owned by our church. I consider it essential to my leadership role that I carve out extended time to be with the Lord and seek His will for our church family. No one else is there. It is a tent-of-meeting time for two—Him and me. I will gladly boast in my weakness and say that I am not a strong enough leader to simply check in with God once or twice a day. I need more than that. I need entire days spent alone with Him without the distraction of food or appointments or messages. Why not try a day away with Him as a leader who is a parent or spouse or businessperson, and see if the next steps on the road do not become clear to you.

Three Checkpoints on a Leader's Path

Along this bit-by-bit, breadcrumb path, I have found three essential checkpoints. The first is my Bible. It is a great place for any leader to begin to discern the will of God, asking, "Is there anything in God's Word that either promotes or prevents this next step?"

1. The Blueprint

The Word of God is the immutable and solid blueprint for every leader. I know that it will either sand me or crush me. The choice is mine—and believe me, I would rather be sanded than crushed. Choosing humility is far better than being humbled. As we lead others toward God, our thoughts and ways need to be sanded and refined. Our pride in our own plans must be sanded away. If we do not submit to this process and allow God to bring us lower in our hearts, we have closed our eyes to the weight of our responsibility. Those whom we lead trust us to take them in the direction God would have us go. They are banking on our ability to discern God's way—and at times their lives and their livelihood depend upon it. Imagine strutting with pride while others follow. What a mockery of God's grace!

The exciting journey of blazing new trails requires guidance from God's Word. Years ago, riders for the Pony Express—an overland mail route that stretched from St. Joseph, Missouri, to Sacramento, California—each carried a full-sized Bible presented to them when they joined up. Despite the rugged, demanding ride and strict weight restrictions (light clothing and saddles, light horse shoes or none at all, flat mail pouches and tissue-thin paper) the riders carried God's Word along with them.[2]

I need to remain under the authority of God's Word. The higher the places of leadership, the more we need to walk in humility. I've often lain face down on the floor and said, "Lord, this is all I've got." I've spoken in front of thousands with a weak outline and a single verse and seen miracles—not because of my wit, but because of His power. Many times, the messages that I thought were my worst God used the most. Leaders, let God's

Word purify your heart and your motives as you guide others. He will never call you to do anything contrary to the principles in His Word. Instead, He will use His Word to guide you when your own thoughts begin to deceive and stray.

Here are just a few portions of His Word that God has used in my life as I lead at home and in the church:

- When I am aggravated and want to force my way on others, I remember that "man's anger does not bring about the righteous life that God desires" (Jas. 1:20). The means are more important to Him than the end.
- When my kids push the boundaries as soon as I set them in place . . . "Fathers, do not embitter your children, or they will become discouraged" (Col. 3:21). When I hear these words, I slow down and realize there is more at stake than whatever immediate issue is at hand.
- When I'm leading, but followers are complaining, God's Word reminds me that "a gentle answer turns away wrath, but a harsh word stirs up anger" (Prov. 15:1). Then I listen and calmly discuss, laying aside the need to defend and strike back.
- When I want to scream, "Come on, people!" to get them behind me, I recall Paul's words: "Follow my example, as I follow the example of Christ" (1 Cor. 11:1).
- When I'm tempted to rehearse why I'm right, and what I'm going to say the next time I am challenged, I hear "In your anger do not sin: Do not let the sun go down while you are still angry" (Eph. 4:26-27), and I say instead, "Lord, I trust You, and I forgive them."

• When I think, *I have to get this done—it's up to me,* I am reminded of Jesus' words: "I am the vine; you are the branches. If a man remains in me and I in him, he will bear much fruit; apart from me you can do nothing" (John 15:5). Not only is it not up to me, but also my efforts are a waste if they are not performed in His strength.

Thankfully, God's words shape ours and keep us from making matters worse when we are frustrated leading the pack. Be reminded that those who know God's Word the best hear God's voice the most.

2. Gut Check

A leader who desires God's best for his followers learns to listen to his gut. I'm not talking about diet here—I'm talking about discernment. Gut checks are key moments on the breadcrumb trail—times when we sense a slight or strong leading in the discernable whisper of God. Time in the tent of meeting and an awareness and obedience to the Word of God help me discern His way, but there are also times when my gut says go or no— and I have learned to listen to those promptings.

I sense a gut check every time I make a parenting decision to prove "I'm the dad and you're the kid." There are times when my response and my child's infraction are not in line; times when another cookie is fine and is not a live-or-die issue.

I've felt gut checks when I've rushed to return a phone call without praying about my response, dialing all but the last digit before hanging up and yielding to the Holy Spirit's conviction to wait and pray it through.

I felt a gut check like acid reflux in my soul when I realized the girl I dated in college was not the one, and I needed to let go so both of us could find the person God meant for us.

Even in godly marriages we can feel that gut check that says, "This issue is not worth the conflict . . . and you need to apologize."

Oh, how much better off we'd be if we learned to listen to and heed those gut checks. How good of God to lead us this way. Wise is the leader who does not ignore his or her gut when it speaks!

God's Word affirms this kind of leading, too:

Whether you turn to the right or to the left, your ears will hear a voice behind you saying, "This is the way; walk in it" (Isa. 30:21).

He guides the humble in what is right and teaches them his way (Ps. 25:9).

This is what the LORD says: "Stand at the crossroads and look; ask for the ancient paths, ask where the good way is, and walk in it, and you will find rest for your souls." But you said, "We will not walk in it" (Jer. 6:16).

As we learn to lead by following, we hear God's direction. Like a dog follows the whistle of its master, we follow our Lord and Master. A hunch might say hire that person, or let someone go. It may seem like a crazy idea, but believing that you are hearing your Master's voice, you obey. This concept is not a license to spiritual attention deficit disorder, or an excuse to follow any whim. A gut check is listening to the Holy Spirit's directing for a sustained movement in your heart that points to honoring God.

He is the counselor of every leader's soul, even without a scheduled appointment. He is not "cousin It" of the Trinity, but the Spirit of the living God at work in us. We must learn to yield to His voice and tune our ear to His leading, asking for clarity instead of suppressing any and every gut check He provides. Too much is riding on our leadership to ignore the promptings of the Holy Spirit. Instead of smothering His guidance, we should be asking for more!

I hope you don't think these things are just for leaders in the church. They're not. They're for every Christ follower, no matter the arena in which he or she leads. There is no line of demarcation that divides the sacred leader from the secular leader based on the field of endeavor. Spending time with God, knowing and obeying His Word and learning to trust our spiritual gut checks are not luxuries for pastor-types. Every leader, every parent and every employer must be spending time with God if he or she hopes to discover where He is leading. What do you imagine God could do with your business, your family, if you intentionally spent time with Him, seeking His wisdom and His way?

God is often more interested in the journey than the destination as He leads us and shapes our character. You will make mistakes and get it wrong sometimes. I will too. Don't beat yourself up. I have come to rest as a leader through valuing the times when I trust God and obey Him, knowing even in my stumbles that I am growing stronger. If my ultimate goal is to always be proved right, I'm in trouble!

We imagine the end or goal as a glorious finish line where a trophy waits inscribed with our name, but God is all about the process. He's got the end taken care of. It's secure. He's concerned with whether we honor and glorify Him along the way. If you're going to fail (and you will), "fail forward" as John Maxwell likes to say. Be moving toward Him, even as you stumble.

3. Opened and Closed Doors

In addition to God's Word, and gut checks, the leader must be looking for doors. If you are at the front of the pack, you're going to come to the door first. Your job is to discern whether the door is for you—whether it is opening or closing. If you are on the right path, you'll encounter doors that are flung open, and doors that slam shut. These doors are directions; they are the Lord's guidance and grace as He builds the narrative of your journey. But whether the doors you encounter are opened or closed, every path of God ends with someone bragging on God's goodness. God is the one who opens and shuts doors, not us.

> These are the words of him who is holy and true, who holds the key of David. What he opens no one can shut, and what he shuts no one can open. I know your deeds. See, I have placed before you an *open door* that no one can shut. I know that you have little strength, yet you have kept my word and have not denied my name (Rev. 3:7-8, emphasis added).

> Now when I went to Troas to preach the gospel of Christ and found that the Lord had *opened a door* for me (2 Cor. 2:12, emphasis added).

When a door closes, feel free to knock on it in prayer, but please don't kick it in. You are not a thief looking to break into a locked house. You are a child of God who is trying to discern the leading of your heavenly Father. Accept both the opened and the closed doors as guidance. If you have spent time with Him, honoring His Word, and if your gut check has led you to the present door, then rest in Him. He is at work . . . and He holds the master key.

The Word of God . . . a personal gut check . . . open and closed doors. These are the checkpoints on the leader's path to knowing God's will. When the next step of His will becomes apparent, then what?

Fulfilling the Vision or Swamped by Projects?

Every leader is a mouthpiece for direction. Leaders must speak the words that guide their followers. Whether those followers are children, colleagues, church members or clients, they cannot be expected to read their leader's mind. Projects can be assigned; vision cannot. Vision must be communicated to be realized—it must be shared by leaders and "caught" by followers.

A leader communicates vision and then establishes the necessary projects to support that vision. A cautionary word here: Vision and projects are purposefully and dangerously intertwined, and the two must not be confused. Vision is the grand direction of God's leading, while projects are the short-term, incremental tasks that are done to arrive at the goal.

Let me illustrate what I mean. Many people have a vision of living in a comfortable, hospitable home that is open to frequent visitors; but it is possible to get caught up in project mode and never achieve the goal of that vision. For example, people buy houses to fix them up, but the fix-up mode never ends. The pressure of perfection from media, friends and neighbors drives them to Home Depot week after week. As a result, the vision of a comfortable, welcoming home is swallowed up in unending renovation projects.

Often the home was envisioned as the locale of frequent gatherings, giving the homeowners a hospitable justification for more square feet. But most of the time there is no one there but the owners of the house, who are juggling the "balls" of cleaning, decorating or repairing. The "honey do" list of projects engulfs the vision. The patio furniture is seldom occupied; the china remains in the cabinet; no one comes over to the house; while the homeowners continue to scurry to finish unending projects.

Instead, the projects should point to the vision: Clean the house to mess it up with a party; use the china so much that you *know* you'll break some; have a tremendous conversation with a loved one on the patio as spring blossoms. Play in the yard with your kids so much that there are worn spots. Right now, our front yard has numerous patches without grass. We refer to them as the pitcher's mound and bases. Numerous times a week we gladly risk broken windows to have a neighborhood ballgame. In this season of life, I'm growing kids, not grass, and the yard proves it. Allow the vision to drive the projects instead of the projects squelching the vision.

A family might have the vision of raising godly, responsible children—a vision that at least in part could be supported by projects like giving children responsibilities around the house, and attending church. Instead, our kids get soaked in media to such an extent that anything that truly builds family seems "boring." So parents shuttle their kids to and from numerous activities and projects without a vision to drive those activities and projects.

I have bad news, there is a slim to none chance that your child is ever going to make a career of the activity you are spending three days a week participating in. Take a second and count how many people you grew up with, or personally know, that play professional sports. Now ask how many people you know who have helped their marriage and their life by walking with Christ. With the scales tipped, why do we hustle our kids to practice instead of church? Amateur sports build character and teamwork, and they are fun, but they aren't intended to provide a vicarious living for the parent. Ask why you are doing what you are doing. The Duke of Wellington convictingly stated, "What amazes me most about American parents is the way they obey their children."[3]

Does the project you are involved in help to fulfill your ultimate vision? A wise leader knows that it is possible to endlessly chase projects and never fulfill the vision. As leaders, we ask God to reveal His will for those we lead, then we clearly communicate the vision to them, tying subsequent projects to that vision. As you do, followers will see and understand how the things they are doing relate to the big picture, and they will have a hand in seeing the vision come to pass.

Keep Sailing, Even When You're Stuck

Determining God's vision for your team is tough; communicating that vision and moving toward it is challenging as well. But perhaps the toughest thing is to keep on moving forward, bit by bit, in spite of hardships, obstacles and setbacks—in other words, to keep sailing.

One of the most inspiring stories of leadership is the story of Sir Ernest Henry Shackleton and his Antarctic expedition on the ship *Endurance* (1914-1917). The ship's name would become ominously synonymous with its journey. Legend has it that Shackleton chose a team of men to crew his ship by placing this ad: "Men wanted for hazardous journey. Small wages, bitter cold, long months of complete darkness, constant danger. Safe return doubtful. Honor and recognition in case of success."

Shackleton's call for explorers practically guaranteed hardship, and hardship was what he and his crew endured. They had barely sailed a month when their ship was caught in a pack of ice. For the next 10 months, they were unable to move until the ice finally crushed the great ship, and it sank.

Shackleton's men did indeed face bitter cold, darkness and danger. The goal of their voyage seemed impossible; survival became their dearest hope. For five-and-a-half months they lived in tents on ice—no ship, little shelter, no cell phones . . . just solid ice to call home. Four of the crew members set out in a smaller vessel for help, and the rest of the crew waited another five months before rescuers came. But not a single man was lost. Everyone survived!

Whether you are experiencing a calm sea or an icy detour, keep moving toward God. Keep sailing toward the vision, growing in your faith, listening for His voice. Tough times will come. "You wait," said Thomas Pynchon in his novel, reflecting on the Endurance, "everyone has an Antarctic."[4]

Even in the midst of those hard times, the leader can trust that God is in the voyage with him, shaping his heart and growing his faith. As you seek His vision in leading others, he will revolutionize your desires as well. Just listen to the words of Moses, who learned to value God above everything else:

> Then Moses said to him, "If your Presence does not go with us, do not send us up from here. How will anyone know that you are pleased with me and with your people unless you go with us? What else will distinguish me and your people from all the other people on the face of the earth?" And the LORD said to Moses, "I will do the very thing you have asked, because I am pleased with you, and I know you by name" (Exod. 33:15-17).

Moses' words reveal the heart of leadership that God desires in His followers. What more could we ask than the promise of His presence?

For Further Reflection and Discussion

1. Who is looking to you for leadership?
2. Describe your "tent of meeting." How do you seek His will for you and for those you lead?
3. What doors do you sense God opening and closing as you seek to lead others?

4. How effective are you at communicating the vision God gives you to your family, your team, your church or organization? Do your followers understand their roles?

5. How have you seen projects swallow vision in your life? Where is that happening today?

Notes

1. S. I. McMillen, *None of These Diseases* (Grand Rapids, MI: Fleming Revell, 1993). http://bible.org/illustration/are-you-leader.

2. P. L. Tan, *Encyclopedia of 7700 Illustrations: A Treasury of Illustrations, Anecdotes, Facts and Quotations for Pastors, Teachers and Christian Workers* (Garland, TX: Bible Communications, 1996).

3. The Duke of Wellington, cited in Tan, *Encyclopedia of 7700 Illustrations.*

4. Thomas Pynchon, *V.* (New York: HarperCollins, 1961), p. 255.

12

LIGHTS OUT

Bam! Zap! Pow! and all of the other Batmanesque cartoon words you can think of described the moment, and then the power went out. New York City came to a screeching halt. Subways stopped, Times Square no longer glowed with neon, the Mets evening game against the Giants was cancelled, the United Nations and Wall Street closed their doors. The largest city in the U.S. was in the dark ages, literally. The newspaper headline the next day simply read "Powerless." That one word said it all. Even with all the state-of-the art technology, and buildings reaching into the clouds, the lack of power resulted in thousands of people walking home from a shortened and purposeless workday. The newspaper front page, like others around the country, pictured masses of men with loosened ties, and barefoot women with high heels in their hands, walking across the Brooklyn Bridge!

New York City residents still had all of the appliances, televisions and light switches they'd had before the storm, but they were now useless. No power, no progress; just sit and wait. The value of buildings in Manhattan was not measured by their size or location, but by the rattle of a generator powering emergency lights.

God's power is a necessary ingredient for us too. Not much happens without it, because true light for our path comes from the power source of Christ. Moses will see this picture in HD through the plagues God sends to the people of Egypt.

Every Christ-follower and every leader can rest assured that God's will has God's power behind it. God's power may be manifested in quiet, steady ways, or in dramatic, you-have-to-see-it-to-believe-it miracles. Moses experienced both, but as he carried out his burning-bush assignment, he came to understand that God's will, done in God's way, has God's power. Always.

Moses made it his business to know the God of God's will. He followed his God from the backside of nowhere to the courts of Pharaoh the same way you and I are called to follow Him: one step at a time. And God did, indeed, demonstrate His power in spectacular ways when Moses came before Pharaoh and said, "This is what the Lord, the God of the Hebrews, says: 'Let my people go, so that they may worship me'" (Exod. 9:1). Why were demonstrations of God's power needed? Because Pharaoh was not inclined to let his nation of slave laborers go. When Moses and Aaron asked for their release, he resisted, just as God predicted he would:

> But I will harden Pharaoh's heart, and though I multiply my miraculous signs and wonders in Egypt, he will not listen to you. Then I will lay my hand on Egypt and with mighty acts of judgment I will bring out my divisions, my people the Israelites. And the Egyptians will know that I am the Lord when I stretch out my hand against Egypt and bring the Israelites out of it (Exod. 7:3-5).

Did God harden Pharaoh's heart, or did Pharaoh harden his own heart? Yes to both. Ten times the Bible says God hardened Pharaoh's heart, and three times it says that Pharaoh hardened his heart. In another five instances, we're simply told that Pharaoh's heart was hardened. In any case, it was that persistent hardness of heart that prompted God's mighty demonstrations of His power through a series of miraculous signs and terrible plagues. Some might argue that these acts were merely coincidental or caused by nature alone, but at least four factors mark the difference between a miraculous sign and a natural phenomenon: timing, location, purpose and prediction. These four factors can determine what is a miracle and what is not. These factors also help us personally determine God's will; so a quick overview of how we know the plagues were miraculous is helpful.

Timing and Purpose

As we'll see when Moses declared the plague of flies, for example, he told Pharaoh, "This miraculous sign will happen tomorrow," and it did. When he said Egypt would be devastated by hail "at this time tomorrow," wouldn't you know it; hail came down at that very hour! This precise and accurate timing indicated not a natural occurrence, but a divinely planned one. We've heard it over and over, and discussed it in detail already: God's timing is perfect. His miraculous timing rained down manna and quail from heaven to feed Moses and his sojourners. God in His perfect timing, through His magnificent power, accomplishes His eternal will.

Also the acts of God's power have a higher purpose that is missing from mere natural phenomena. When Jesus walked on water, He did not do so to prove that He could float! He walked on water to demonstrate the power of God—that God could do anything He purposed, regardless of the laws of matter. When He rose from the dead, it wasn't a carnival trick, but a permanent defeat of death and sin. God's miracles have a purpose—they are not just a freak show phenomenon. The "why" of miracles and of the plagues was to declare the greatness of God.

We must possess a personal understanding of this. The miracle of God's guidance in our lives is not simply to bless us. We can easily slip into thinking that God's guidance is solely for our own pleasure. But when God is at work opening and closing doors, our lives shine with His greatness for others to see. We aren't the recipients of the miracle as much as we are the vehicles for it. Like a boomerang, it comes from Him through us, and back to Him.

Miracles are a combination of a Father lovingly blessing His children and showing His power to others. We are thankful for the blessing but realize the purpose is higher than our perspective. In fact, He said so Himself in the message He gave Moses to deliver to Pharaoh: "Let my people go, so that they may worship me, or this time I will send the full force of my plagues against you and your officials and your people, *so you may know that there is no one like me in all the earth*" (Exod. 9:13-14, emphasis added).

Prediction and Location

Finally, Moses predicted all of these things. He did not just state them after the fact; he clearly said, here's the timing, the location and the purpose of each miracle—all *before* they happened. The prophetic declaration of the future is something God uses to establish credibility throughout the Bible. In just the case of Jesus alone, more than 300 prophecies were stated before He ever took a breath of earth's air. His birth, life, death and second coming are all documented in the Old Testament, hundreds or thousands of years before the manger.

Imagine if the five o'clock news were to announce that it would soon rain in one spot but not in another one nearby, or that the rain would fall for exactly eight minutes at 2:00 P.M., and then stop. Or, that of a dozen people on a sidewalk, rain would fall on only three of them—and then the anchorman told you which three! If these things did in fact happen as predicted, you would be less likely to attribute them to chance. Instead, you would very likely think the station possessed some supernatural power, and you would probably pay close attention to the next thing they said. The timing, location, purpose and prediction of the 10 plagues show that this is God's power at work through Moses.

The plagues were specifically predicted in location, not randomly experienced. Basically, they affected the Egyptians, not the Jews. The hailstorm struck throughout Egypt—everywhere but Goshen, where the Israelites lived. The plague of darkness covered all Egypt for three days so that "no one could see anyone else or leave his place," but "all the Israelites had light in the places where they lived" (Exod. 10:23). With the exactness of a GPS co-ordinate, the missiles of each plague struck on a dime.

These things can give us assurance on our burning-bush journey as well. God is in the know, even when we don't have a clue. Right now, especially as you are reading a book like this, God is orchestrating opportunities for you to discover Him more deeply. Tomorrow and the day after that may create a crossroads for you, presenting a choice to be selfless or selfish. Will you pay enough attention to notice? A decision is headed your way that the slip of paper in your last fortune cookie cannot adequately prepare you for. That decision is not a surprise to God. His timing, location, purpose and knowledge are acting in unison to lead you another step. His will always comes with His power.

Moses trusted God's timing, location, purpose and ability to predict the future. But will we take what we've seen and trust Him for our future? Corrie ten Boom wisely said, "Never be afraid to trust an unknown future to a known God." The God we seek daily knows daily what is ahead. Understanding what makes a miracle miraculous helps us indentify God's work in our lives. Personalizing these truths is the key to changing our day's headline from "Powerless" to "Powerful."

For Further Reflection and Discussion

1. Why is God's power crucial to living a life of purpose?
2. Which of the four credentials of Moses' miracles amazes you the most: timing, location, purpose or ability to predict?
3. How is a blackout or power failure similar to living life in your own strength?
4. In what area of your life are you trusting in your own power instead of God's?

13

Tenth Round
Knockout

Imagine a Las Vegas boxing match between Pharaoh and God: "In the blue corner, the emperor of Egypt, the sultan of slave labor, the boxer of bricks without straw, fighting in his own power and wisdom—a featherweight in reality, but a heavyweight in his own mind . . . Pharaooooh!" (Insert canned wild applause track.)

"In the other corner, the Creator of creation, the one who remembers Pharaoh in diapers and knows the day of his death, boxing through his servant Moses; He floats like a butterfly and created the bee—the heaviest of heavyweights . . . GOD ALMIGHTYYYY!" (Insert complete and utter universe-wide silence and awe.)

The scene is set for us in this chapter to see the power of God—the power that accompanies His plan; the power we have access to in this life. If we rest in His power, His will in our life goes forward; but if we rebel against His power . . . no power, no progress.

The series of plagues that came upon Pharaoh and Egypt will teach us three things. The first set of these powerful, supernatural acts declares God's mighty presence. The second set shows His divine providence in all things. The third set demonstrates His awesome power over all of life. We need His presence, providence and power in our lives, as well. Notice the intricacies of God's assault upon the false gods of Egypt. There is a deeper reason and rhyme here than just disaster. As always with God, His ways are carefully calculated.

His Presence
Plagues 1 to 3: Blood, Frogs and Gnats

Pharaoh's heart was already unyielding and hard against Moses, Aaron, the Israelites and their God when the series of supernatural plagues began. They had asked Pharaoh to let them leave. He had refused to let them go. Perhaps he doubted the presence of their God, or he believed that God was nothing to be feared or respected. When Pharaoh said no, God said to Moses:

> Tell Aaron, "Take your staff and stretch out your hand over the waters of Egypt—over the streams and canals, over the ponds and all the reservoirs—and they will turn to blood. Blood will be everywhere in Egypt, even in the wooden buckets and stone jars" (Exod. 7:19).

Pharaoh believed that he was the "god" of the Nile River, but he soon learned that Moses' God had a more powerful presence in Egypt. When Aaron stretched out his staff, the waters of the Nile turned to blood. Fish died. The smell of death pervaded everything. Not only did the water of the river turn to blood, but water standing in pots and buckets and jars did too.

The apostle Paul, in his letter to the church at Corinth, said that those who believe are an aroma of death to those who do not believe (see 2 Cor. 2:15). Pharaoh did not believe in the God of Israel . . . and all around him was the smell of death. God's supernatural turning of the waters of Egypt to blood demonstrated His presence in Egypt and His power over the lifeblood of the Egyptians. But when Pharaoh's magicians mimicked the miracle, using their "secret arts," his heart became hard and he refused Moses and Aaron.

The drama didn't stop there. The plague of blood was followed seven days later by a proliferation of frogs after Moses again demanded the Israelites' release, and Pharaoh again refused. The Egyptians worshiped a goddess named Heqet, a symbol of fertility with the body of a woman and the head of a frog. In a supernatural act to "trump" Heqet, God made the Nile River teem with frogs. Frogs covered the land, too, crawling into Pharaoh's palace and into the houses and beds and kneading bowls of the Egyptians. It was as if God was saying, "Attention, Heqet-worshiping Egyptians: you want frogs? I'll give you frogs." And He did.

Pharaoh's magicians duplicated this plague, too; but after they did, Pharaoh called for Moses and Aaron and asked them to pray to their God to get rid of the frogs! He may not have been willing to obey God, but he acknowledged His existence! As asked, Moses prayed for the frogs to be gone the next day, and they were. Relieved, Pharaoh rescinded his promise to let the Israelites go. Dead frogs were piled into heaps and the land reeked from their rotting bodies, but Pharaoh's no was firm. Round two ended in a standoff.

The third plague that confirmed God's presence was a plague of gnats—tiny insects that filled the air and covered men and animals like a fine dust. Again Pharaoh summoned his magicians to imitate the awful miracle, but they could not. Instead, they confessed to Pharaoh, "This is the finger of God" (Exod. 8:19). Pharaoh heard, but he did not listen and heed. His heart was too hard to bow to the God whose presence he could no longer doubt.

Plague	Purpose	Egyptian God Deposed
1. Nile to Blood	Showed God's power over the Egyptians' life source	Hapi, god of the Nile
2. Frogs	Showed God's power over the Egyptians' fertility	Heqet, goddess of birth, who had a frog's head
3. Gnats	Showed God's power over the magicians— they could not replicate it	Set, god of the desert

These plagues of blood, frogs and gnats confirmed God's presence in Egypt, and His power over Egyptian magic and Egyptian gods. God's will has God's presence. Do you sense His presence as you try to discern His will? Sometimes we aren't sure He's with us. We cry out and say, "God, are You here?" We don't always feel that presence, even though we trust in it. But there are other times when His presence is almost palpable— when He seems near enough to touch.

I experienced one of those times during an ordinary lunch appointment at Rice University. As I stood in line at the Faculty Club, eyeing all the great food, I strongly sensed God's presence. He wasn't telling me to watch my cholesterol or skip the cornbread (thank goodness); I just experienced His nearness to me and acknowledged it by saying in my heart, *Lord, I sense You here, and I love You. I give You my life today, and all that I am. I give You this lunch meeting to use for Your purposes. I give You everything. You are my God.* Nothing outwardly miraculous happened. He simply confirmed for me that He was with me—even in a noisy dining room on a college campus.

Do you ever sense His presence? If you don't, you may need to examine your walk with Christ—because if you are a believer in Christ, He lives in you. It isn't a matter of proximity but intimacy. Since He lives in you, you should experience His presence. If you seldom or never do, ask yourself if your "relationship" with Him is real, or if it just rule-keeping or a Sunday-only kind of thing. I can confirm for many men that the lack of sensing His presence is the result of flat out laziness in seeking it. God's presence is a part of His will, and His will is accompanied by His power. It's not the show-and-tell, hocus-pocus miracles you're after; it's the loving embrace of a Father. It's His presence. His will is with you.

A. W. Tozer described God's presence like this: "The revelation of God to any man is not God coming from a distance once upon a time to pay a brief and momentous visit to the man's soul. . . . It is not a matter of miles but experience."[1]

King David experienced God's presence in a real way. "Where can I go from your Spirit?" he asked. "Where can I flee from your presence? If I go up to the heavens, you are there; if I make my bed in the depths, you are there. If I rise on the wings of the dawn, if I settle on the far side of the sea, even there your hand will guide me, your right hand will hold me fast" (Ps. 139:7-10). Be attentive and expectant for it, because God's will is always marked by His presence. "In your presence there is fullness of joy; at your right hand are pleasures forevermore" (Ps. 16:11, *ESV*).

His Providence
Plagues 4 to 6: Flies, Livestock and Boils

God's power is also demonstrated in His providence. What is providence? It is overseeing guidance and direction. God's providence means that His hand guides the nations, mankind and the times. Pharaoh might have believed that providence was *his* realm; God showed him otherwise with three more plagues.

Soon after the gnats descended, more insects plagued Egypt: "Dense swarms of flies poured into Pharaoh's palace and into the houses of his officials, and throughout Egypt the land was ruined by the flies" (Exod. 8:24). They were everywhere; except in the land of Goshen, among God's people. There were no swarms of flies in Goshen. "I will make a distinction," God said, "between my people and your people" (Exod. 8:23). And He did. Have you ever tried to swat a fly? They go every which way, and there seems to be no logic to where they land. But these flies distinguished between Egyptians and Israelites, between Egyptian and Israelite homes. In His providence, God caused a terrible plague to thwart one people and spare another.

The Lord's supreme ability to distinguish shows His care for His people. Every business in your industry may be declining, but if God wills it, yours could be on the upswing. Conversely, while others soar, God may have you crawl in order to show you something that can't be found in the clouds.

Pharaoh summoned Moses and offered this compromise: "Go, sacrifice to your God here in the land" (Exod. 8:25). In other words, Pharaoh was saying that they could worship their God, but they had to do so there in Egypt, as slaves. Moses declined: "We must take a three-day journey into the desert to offer sacrifices to the LORD our God, as he commands us" (v. 27). Pharaoh refused the three-day journey of consequence, and instead offered another compromise: "I will let you go . . . but you must not go very far" (v. 28). Then he asked Moses to pray for him! Moses prayed, and the flies left—every last one. But Pharaoh hardened his heart, and the plagues that demonstrated God's providence were not yet complete.

Next, God's hand struck the livestock in the fields of Egypt with hail: horses, donkeys, camels, cattle, sheep and goats. In an agrarian society, wealth was measured in livestock. Moses told Pharaoh that if he did not let the Israelites go, God would bring a terrible plague on the livestock grazing in Egyptian fields—but no animal belonging to the Israelites would die. God set a deadline, but Pharaoh let it pass. The next day, "All the livestock of the Egyptians died, but not one animal belonging to the Israelites died" (Exod. 9:6). Economic disaster resulted, and once again the gods of Egypt proved no match for the provident God of Israel. His hand controlled wealth—something Pharaoh no doubt believed was under *his* control. Even so, "His heart was unyielding and he would not let the people go" (Exod. 9:7).

As Pharaoh's heart became harder, the plagues became more intense and personal. Next, God instructed Moses to toss dust from the furnace into the air, and as a result, horrible boils or sores broke out on men and animals. (Note: The animals here may have been those not "in the fields" during the previous plague, but instead kept in barn-like shelters.) The magicians of Pharaoh's court were helpless. They could do nothing. Egypt's little-g gods were useless in ensuring the health of the nation. But still Pharaoh refused to let God's people go.

Plague	Purpose	Egyptian God Deposed
4. Flies	To discriminate between the Hebrews and the Egyptians	Uatchit, a god possibly represented by a fly
5. Livestock	To show God's power over the Egyptians' wealth	Hathor, goddess with a cow's head
6. Boils	To show God's power over human illness and the magicians	Sekhmet, goddess with power over disease

God is provident over our wealth and our health. His will prevails. Do you understand the providence of God in your life? You may work hard and work smart and have impeccable credentials, but God determines whether or not you will advance. "In his heart a man plans his course," wrote King Solomon, "but the LORD determines his steps" (Prov. 16:9). The providence of God's hand moves us and moves the events of history.

Have you stretched beyond your own understanding and begun to trust in His? You can do everything "right" and succeed. You can do everything "right" and fail. God's providence is over and above all and goes beyond human understanding.

So much of life is flat-out unexplainable. Why our life turns the corners it does is beyond figuring out. Only the providence of God can give explanation to the twists that leave us scratching our heads. Some people derail faith by throwing a penalty flag on God's actions, while others learn to embrace whatever He brings. Those who derail unknowingly claim with their attitude and actions to know more than they do. To the contrary, those who embrace find comfort in letting a trusted Guide lead the way.

Joel and Emily Skaggs are embracers. With a beautiful little girl already, and another child on the way, Emily's OB appointments were routine, until one test. Suddenly their preparation wasn't just about outfitting the nursery and folding cute clothes; it was about considering the possibility of a little boy with Down syndrome. When Seth arrived, and the diagnosis was confirmed, my wife and I, along with another couple, drove to the hospital to congratulate Joel and Emily. As we entered the room and sat down, we all teared up with a strange combination of joy and sadness. We cried for the joy of a new life and grieved for the challenge of a new reality. The providence of God lets you do both. It is so solid that you can lean upon it in seemingly different directions yet remain on solid footing.

Joel and Emily were confident of their initial decision (which truly wasn't even a decision) to continue the pregnancy. We live in a parental "Achieve-atron" society, and we've even applied that to the womb. Our society incorrectly equates a child's ability with a child's worth. Today, if someone finds out that their baby shows any sign of being less-than-perfect (if "perfect" can be defined), abortion is considered a viable option. A full 90 percent of babies determined to have Down syndrome in the womb are aborted. Providence doesn't do that, and therefore keeps babies alive. Realizing God is in control means that we can walk through the challenge and believe every child is a gift. As Augustine said, "Trust the past to God's mercy, the present to God's love and the future to God's providence."

"We knew life would be different from here and we grieved. We knew life would be different from here and we celebrated," the Skaggs said. God created Seth perfectly and for a purpose. Embracers receive that, even if they don't prefer it. They realize that a higher plan is in motion that must not be derailed. I submit to you that God uses special-needs children (and those with illnesses, too) as a tool to unlock hearts. Even the hardest of hearts seems to soften at the opportunity to watch the journey of a child like Seth.

The Skaggs embraced the providence of God, knowing that in His sovereignty He chose their family to receive the blessing of Seth. It wasn't an accident, a defect or a handicap. Their other children will have a bottomless heart of compassion that will take years to form in the rest of us. As parents, they will struggle as we all do, but sweetness will blossom in their marriage too. Seth is my little buddy at church. High fives and hugs are our connections as the Lord has used him to teach me about His providence.

Pharaoh should have learned of God's sovereignty through the first six plagues, but . . . *ding!* Round 6 is complete, and he staggers back to his corner.

His Power
Plagues 7 to 9: Hail, Locusts and Darkness

The first three plagues demonstrated God's presence in Egypt. The second set of plagues was evidence of His providence over all of life. The third set of plagues was the most powerful of all. Violent storms ravaged Egypt, ripping the land apart. Then locusts swarmed and devoured what little was left. After the storms and the locusts, darkness settled over the land for three days.

Modern meteorologists predict our strongest storms—but they cannot control them. In my city, weathermen work overtime during hurricane season, spotting potential storms and reporting on their course and intensity, but these forecasters can't keep a hurricane from forming or to steer its path once it is formed. They don't have that kind of power.

As Pharaoh's resistance grew even stronger, Moses predicted a "category five" storm: "At this time tomorrow I will send the worst hailstorm that has ever fallen on Egypt, from the day it was founded until now" (Exod. 9:18). Some of Pharaoh's officials began preparing for the big storm when they heard Moses' words—they had seen what his God could do. But Pharaoh did not let the Israelites go, and the storm headed straight for Egypt just as God said it would.

The Egyptians had a "weather" god, too—a sky goddess named Nut. (Seems like you would wise up when your god is named Nut, but they didn't.) No doubt, Pharaoh's magicians called on Nut to control the storm, but their efforts were futile. They probably cried to Osiris, the Egyptian god of crops, too, but he proved useless to protect the fields of Egypt from blistering hail. Set, the storm god, had no power to stop this storm either. The little-g gods of Egypt were no matches for Almighty God. He alone controlled the weather—and why not? He made the winds and rain and hail.

When Jesus and His disciples encountered a violent storm centuries later on the Sea of Galilee, Jesus shouted for the winds to cease, and they did. His disciples wondered at this, saying, "What kind of man is this? Even the winds and the waves obey Him!" (Matt. 8:27). They could see that His power was like nothing they'd ever seen before, and it filled them with amazement and awe.

God had a purpose in sending the storm to Egypt, and it was not only to force Pharaoh's hand to release the Israelites. He had a bigger agenda than that. He meant for Pharaoh and all of Egypt to know "that there is no one like me in all the earth" (Exod. 9:14). In fact, God declared that He had raised up Pharaoh just for this purpose: "That I might show you my power and that my name might be proclaimed in all the earth" (v. 16). God was making a name for Himself, and all Pharaoh and the Egyptians could do was hide and watch as hail fell from the sky, beat down the vegetation and killed everything that was not sheltered. It did not rain hail in the land of Goshen. And Pharaoh did not release the Israelites. Are you surprised?

Before the next plague, God reminded Moses that He had hardened Pharaoh's heart, and that more disaster was yet to come. But He also shared His reason for doing so: "That I may perform these miraculous signs of mine among them and that you may tell your children and grandchildren how I dealt harshly with the Egyptians and how I performed my signs among them, and that you may know that I am the LORD" (Exod. 10:1-2). God wanted the Israelites to witness the awful plague of locusts, and tell their children and grandchildren how God stripped Egypt bare. He wanted them to tell the story of His power and greatness, from generation to generation.

Does your heart beat for the future of God's people, or are you so concerned with your own small corner of history that you can't see the importance of the parts of His story yet to come? Do you tell your children about the way God has worked in days past, and in your own life? Do you invest them with the great story of His redemptive plan, so that it can still be told long after you are gone? Oh, that we would be about telling the next generation of the power of God!

When Moses predicted the plague of locusts, instead of cutting his losses and relenting, Pharaoh tried again to strike a deal with Moses and with Israel's God. Have you ever imagined that you could strike a deal with God for partial obedience? That you could get Him to settle for less than what He has asked of you? That your yes or no might be the final word on anything?

Partial obedience is usually mitigated disobedience. Trusting God's leading doesn't mean fanatically leaping off the edge; neither does it mean that we can partially step off. We are to be listeners, not deal makers with God. Moses' request was clear as crystal, yet even after numerous plagues, Pharaoh thought he had bargaining chips left on the table. His officials pleaded with him to relent when they heard Moses' prediction, saying, "Let the people go, so that they may worship the LORD their God. Do you not yet realize that Egypt is ruined?" (Exod. 10:7). But the sultan of slaves would not relent, and he waited for the bell to ring for the ninth round.

Pharaoh's next ante was the suggestion that Moses might take only the men out of Egypt, leaving the women and children behind. When Moses replied that everyone—men, women and children—was to leave Egypt, Pharaoh refused and drove Moses and Aaron out of his presence. Moses understood that following God's instruction for Israel was an "all or nothing" deal, even if Pharaoh did not. Then at God's command, Moses stretched out his hand over Egypt and great clouds of locusts swarmed, devouring everything in the fields and covering the ground until it was black and until nothing green remained in the land.

Then came the ninth plague . . . darkness. This time Moses did not give Pharaoh a warning of what God was about to do. Instead, darkness so complete and deep fell that the Egyptian sun god Re was buried in it. For three days not a glimmer of light remained, as if God said, "Go for it, Mr. Egyptian sun god; let's see what you've got." And Re had nothing at all to match the power of God. This blackout was a rifle shot to the heart of the Egyptian gods, of which Re was considered the chief god, and Pharaoh his representative. Now in darkness far worse than New York City's blackout, Re was revealed as false. Therefore, Pharaoh summoned Moses and told him to leave with all the men, women and children—but to leave his livestock behind. Moses refused. Isn't Pharaoh beginning to look desperate?

"Young man, young man, your arm is too short to box with God."[2] He's a dealer with nothing to deal, but he keeps trying to bargain with God! (Of course, you or I would never do anything so futile and silly, right?) We're not told that Moses prayed for light to be restored in Egypt after three days of darkness, but we are told that the Israelite's were never in the dark.

As believers in Christ, it is God's will that we would shine. Matthew 5:16 says, "Let your light shine before men, that they may see your good deeds and praise your Father in heaven." The power of God shining through your life differentiates you from other people. The most attractive thing about a godly woman can't be bought at a makeup counter in the mall; it is a shining light in her eyes. A man of respect is not created through achievements but from a character that reflects brightly the light of Christ. When we allow God's power to have control, we are like a single building with electricity in the midst of darkness.

Plague	Purpose	Egyptian God Deposed
7. Hail	To show God's power over the weather and the crops	Nut, the sky goddess; Osiris, god of crop fertility; Set, god of storms
8. Locusts	To declare God's power to the next generation	Nut, the sky goddess; Osiris, god of crop fertility
9. Darkness	To show God's power over the heavens—particularly the sun and moon	Re, the sun god (the chief Egyptian god that was represented in Pharaoh)

Knockout Punch
Plague 10: Death of the Firstborn

God told Moses that He had one final plague in store for Egypt . . . and this was the greatest demonstration yet of His mighty power. The plagues that had so far visited the water and air and land of Egypt were about to invade *every single home* and take something irreplaceable from it: the life of every firstborn son. This plague would attest to God's power over life and death, and no Egyptian household would be spared. This time no hope remained of avoiding the consequences of disaster. The consequences would be devastatingly complete:

> About midnight, I will go throughout Egypt. Every firstborn son in Egypt will die, from the firstborn son of Pharaoh, who sits on the throne, to the firstborn son of the slave girl, who is at her hand mill, and all the firstborn of the cattle as well. There will be a loud wailing throughout Egypt—worse than there has ever been or ever will be again. But among the Israelites, not a dog will bark at any man or animal. Then you will know that the LORD makes a distinction between Egypt and Israel. All these officials of yours will come to me, bowing down before me and saying, "Go, you and all the people who follow you!" After that I will leave (Exod. 11:4-8).

The next morning, every home of the Egyptians found every firstborn son lifeless. Only once in my life have I heard the cries of a freshly grieving mother. Logs from a huge bonfire had fallen at Texas A&M University, killing 12 students. I was in the hospital waiting room with friends and family of the victims. A mom of a deceased student entered the room and, well, I don't ever want to hear a cry like that again. It pierces places in you that are so deep you didn't know they existed. That kind of cry, that kind of wail, was heard in every home throughout Egypt.

If Pharaoh had listened somewhere along the way, it wouldn't have come to this. But he didn't.

Plague	Purpose	Egyptian God Deposed
10. Death of firstborn	To reveal God's power as the giver of life	Min, god of reproduction; Pharaoh's firstborn son, thought to be a god

That tenth plague was a knockout, and Israel was not to slink out of the land of Egypt in fear. Oh, no! They were to leave the land of their slavery with all their own possessions, and many of those of the Egyptians. In chapter 4, we hammered home the point that *God's will never lacks God's supply*. Never was this more apparent than when the Hebrews were given clothing, silver and gold as they exited Egypt.

Ten increasingly awful plagues demonstrated God's power to Pharaoh and the Egyptians, and also to the Israelites. God had power over the sky, the wind, the earth, livestock, human health, wealth and even life and death. That's some power! And that same power of God is invested in His will for us. His power always accompanies His will. He can do the miraculous.

Remember my little friend Seth? God's power is already shining in his life. Down syndrome had affected his hearing, but God's power had a plan. I'll let Emily, his mom, tell you in her own words:

Joel and I were disappointed that he only had hearing in one ear, but we started praying, "Lord, we ask that You would heal Seth's ear if it would bring You much glory. You are able, and we will love You and trust Your will above ours no matter what You choose to do in his life." And so this was our prayer for the next six months. I prayed it so many times that it seemed to roll off my tongue like a child's blessing before a meal, "God is great, God is good . . ." I shared our prayer with several people over the course of time. One of the friends in the church's choir shared it with her daughters who then just said, "Mommy, we need to pray for Seth's miracle ear!" I loved that and then started calling it his "miracle ear" too.

We were called back to the doctor, a kind man about the age of my parents, with a "let's get down to business but have a little fun while we're doing it" attitude. While he combed through Seth's extensive chart, I told him that I wanted a hearing test on both ears. Yes, I knew that the chart shows that he has profound hearing loss in his left ear, but I told him that for six months I'd been praying and asking God for a miracle. I believed that God could still perform miracles if He chose to do so; and that if it wasn't today, I'd continue to want both ears tested each time we came in for checkups. He couldn't argue with me and said, "Sure thing! We'll do it. Why not?" Then he proceeded to give Seth numerous tests.

After Seth passed them all, the doctor and I looked at each other for a moment, and I felt tears forming. "Tell me more, Dr. Allen!" I said to him, more shocked that anything. "Well, momma," the doctor said, "he can hear! Seth got a miracle."[3]

God's will is always accompanied by God's power. The plagues show God's presence, providence and power to accomplish His will in our lives. Big ears are beautiful, but a BIG God is spectacular!

For Further Reflection and Discussion

1. What are your thoughts on the plagues? Too much, or don't mess with God?

2. Do you ever bargain with God, offering partial obedience when He requires full obedience? Can you give an example?

3. Tell a story about a "Seth" you know of. How has this story impacted you and others?

4. How do the 10 plagues illustrate the statement, "God's will is accompanied by God's power"?

Notes

1. A. W. Tozer, *The Pursuit of God* (Radford, VA: Wilder Publications, 2008), p. 44.

2. James Weldon Johnson, The Prodigal Son in God's Trombones: Seven Negro Sermons in Verse, 1927.

2. Joel Skaggs, "Miracle Ear," The Fun House, January 5, 2010. http://skaggsportal.typepad.com/my_weblog/2010/01/miracle-ear.html.

14

EAT, RUN AND
REMEMBER

Americans who were alive on September 11, 2001, will never forget that awful day in our country's history. We can tell you where we were when we heard that terrorists had simultaneously hijacked four planes; the tragic images we saw when we turned on the news; the stories of heroism we learned about in the terrible aftermath of 9/11. One unforgettable story involved United Airlines Flight 93, scheduled to fly from Newark, New Jersey, to San Francisco, California, and a young man named Todd Beamer.

Todd was one of several passengers and crew who placed credit card calls to loved ones when their flight was hijacked. Todd was unable to reach his wife, Lisa, but from emergency operator Lisa Jefferson he learned of the three planes flown into the World Trade Center and the Pentagon. He and a handful of other passengers decided that flight 93 would *not* reach its intended target of destruction, thought to be the White House or Capitol, and took matters into their own hands. Still on the line with the operator, Todd told her of their plan to wrest control of the plane from the hijackers who had stormed the cockpit. The last words she heard as she remained on the line were Todd's: "Are you guys ready? *Let's roll.*"

Flight 93 crashed in a field near Shanksville, Pennsylvania, at 10:03 A.M., 125 miles from Washington, DC. Todd and all the other passengers on board perished. Although no one can be sure of exactly what happened after Todd's determined call to action, one thing is certain: by their bravery, the heroes who joined him that day prevented hundreds if not thousands more deaths. "Let's roll!" became the brave battle cry in the ensuing war on terror. It was a passionate petition for movement.

We've seen that knowing God's will requires a process of discovery, deliberation and discernment . . . but as the heroes of Flight 93 demonstrated, it ultimately requires *action* on our part. The time will come when we must move out and go for it based on what we've learned.

Our exploration of God's will, with Moses as our example, has taken us from a burning bush to a plea of "Let my people go" to a series of mighty miracles done on Israel's behalf. God's will is always accompanied by God's power. And these mighty miracles culminated with one final plague that brought death to every house in Egypt but passed over Israel by a special sign and a meal of memory still eaten today:

This is how you are to eat it [this Passover meal]: with your cloak tucked into your belt, your sandals on your feet and your staff in your hand. Eat it in haste; it is the LORD's Passover. On that same night I will pass through Egypt and strike down every firstborn—both men and animals—and I will bring judgment on all the gods of Egypt. I am the LORD. The blood will be a sign for you on the houses where you are; and when I see the blood, I will pass over you. No destructive plague will touch you when I strike Egypt. This is a day you are to commemorate; for the generations to come you shall celebrate it as a festival to the LORD—a lasting ordinance (Exod. 12:11-14).

God's final blow against Pharaoh and Egypt was to send an angel of death into every Egyptian home, killing every firstborn man, woman, child and animal. But by a special provision—the blood of a lamb placed upon the doorposts of the house—He spared from death the Israelites' firstborn. This special provision was a precursor to the gospel of Jesus—to the blood of Jesus on the cross that would remove the penalty of death from us.

Prior to sending the death angel, God instructed the Israelites to prepare and eat a symbolic meal. The way they were to eat it demonstrated their readiness to move. They were to "eat in haste"—ready to roll.

God's Will Requires Movement

"Tuck your cloak into your belt," God told them, "and keep your shoes on and your staff in hand." Pulling the ends of their robes up and away from their feet meant that they were ready to run. The staff God told them to hold in one hand as they ate was used to fend off wild animals and to climb up steep and rocky inclines, a clue that they wouldn't be in the house long.

The Israelites were also instructed to keep their shoes on as they ate—another hint that this would not be a meal like any other. Meals in this culture were typically long, drawn-out affairs, where the diners would take off their shoes, recline and relax. This meal, in contrast, was to be eaten quickly as they prepared to dash off at a moment's notice.

Notice, too, that this meal was taken in community. Every household was to roast a lamb and eat it together. They may have been told to eat the meal in haste, but they were meant to do so in community. God's will may be discovered individually, but it is meant to be lived out in community. Our church's vision is to be "a relevant Biblical *community*." We want to do life together, getting to know each other, encouraging and depending upon one another.

For that first Passover, families ate together. If one family did not have a lamb to sacrifice, they gathered with another family that did. They roasted the lamb and ate it together, and no doubt bonded over that experience. If you're imagining that you will discover God's will for your life in a way that involves no one but you, perhaps you should reconsider. The nurture and support and positive peer pressure that come from community are essential to all of us. If you don't already, you should pray for your children's friends or your grandchildren's friends to become heartfelt, passionate followers of Jesus Christ. I've made my share of bad decisions because of what my friends would think, haven't you? The community we're surrounded by can make or break us when it's time to roll.

Unfortunately, many of us have many acquaintances but few friends. Community is more than living across the street or working in the adjoining cubicle; it means really knowing someone—not just the superficial, but also the inner good and bad. This type of relationship is not based on hobbies or interests, but on time, trust and forgiveness. You are not really friends until you have forgiven. We are a flawed bunch who sand in the wrong direction at times. So a community or a household that dines together, ready to run at God's command, must be tight enough to need and to forgive one another. Spending time in community means making mistakes, and making mistakes means needing forgiveness.

The telephone operator who spoke with Todd Beamer on September 11 said that his voice was calm and that before he and his seatmates stormed the cockpit, he asked her to recite the Lord's Prayer and the Twenty-third Psalm with him. When they were done, he asked her if she would call his wife and two sons, ages 3 and 1 year, and she said she would. Then Todd quietly and confidently said, "Let's roll." Calm confidence comes when we've waited on God to do His part and have been obedient to His instructions to us. The Israelites had their robes tucked in, their shoes on their feet and their staffs in hand. They had their family and friends around them as they stood ready to move. Chaos and destruction surrounded them, but in their households they remained calm, secure in the knowledge that they were in God's hands, and were a part of His bigger plan.

The events of 9/11 burned themselves into our national consciousness. No one had to tell those of us who witnessed it that the day was hugely significant. Books were written by survivors and by those who lost loved ones on that day, as Lisa Beamer did. Their stories have become part of our history, and generations of

Americans who were not alive on that day will learn of them. God instructed the Israelites to tell the story of the Passover and their dramatic exodus from Egypt. "This is a day you are to commemorate," He said, "for the generations to come you shall celebrate it as a festival to the LORD" (Exod. 12:14).

When a person lives out God's will, his or her obedience becomes a part of the history God is writing. We remember those who move out in faith; those first steps of bravery are spoken about for generations. We may not hear about how neat great-granddad's yard looked, or how uncle so-and-so kept a tidy desk, but we *do* still hear the stories of ancestors who risked everything they had to come to a new land, arriving with nothing more than the clothes on their backs, or of how they resisted oppression, trusting God for help.

Some of these ancestors may have been the first in their clan to follow God—or maybe *you* will be the first God-follower in your own family line. If so, you can be the new "domino"—the one that helps a long line of others come to know the living God. How great to be remembered as the man or woman who started a chain reaction of belief so that others might know the Lord! Your readiness to roll, your willingness to move out for God, might just be a turning point for future generations. Yours could be the story they tell again and again to inspire and encourage one another. I'm the first pastor in my lineage, but I pray I'm not the last.

Pass It Down

God instructed the Israelites to tell the story of that night, because stories have power, and words have power. If I ever doubted it, my first T-ball coaching experience convinced me.

Before every game, right after our warm-up, we would huddle on the pitcher's mound with the other team and we would all "take a knee." Then the other coaches and I would ask the kids to take their hats off, and we'd invite someone to give the opening prayer. When we asked for volunteers, every hand would shoot up. Then when we'd call on one, they'd usually say, "Uh, ummm, okay. What am I doing again?" But once they had the plan, the prayers they prayed spoke volumes. I mean, it was amazing what you heard in these little guys' prayers: "Lord, I pray You will bless this food to the nourishment of our bodies." (Did we promise them *snacks* before the game? I don't remember saying anything about snacks. And what kid uses the word "nourishment" in a sentence?) But what they were doing was repeating prayers they'd heard at home. They were praying what they'd heard their parents pray! It was amazing to realize the influence of the words they'd heard over and over. What our children hear us say will likely become part of their own vocabulary; and what they see us do will likely become second nature to them. (Scary, I know.)

When God instructed the Israelites, "Teach this to your kids," it was because He understood the power of repeated words, and because He knew a day would come when another generation would need to be "ready to roll." Let me ask you, what words do you repeat? What story are you telling with your life? Are you a complainer? Will that be your legacy? Will your children say, "Oh, old Grandpa—he was never satisfied, he was always upset about something." Or will they say, "Yeah, we remember Granddad. He was always ready to go when God said move. He followed God."

God's Will Requires Sacrifice

God performed mighty miracles on Israel's behalf. He broke Pharaoh's resistance with 10 increasingly horrible plagues so that he would release the Israelites from slavery and let them go. But something was required of God's people as well. They were commanded to take a lamb and sacrifice it. And not just any lamb. They were to sacrifice a year-old lamb without defects—in other words, their best. Following God cost them something, and the meal they ate (and would continue to eat in memory of that night) signified that fact. The Passover meal today still symbolizes sacrifice.

The elements of the Passover meal have not changed in thousands of years. Your Jewish friends eat a meal identical to the one consumed the night the death angel visited Egypt. Each element of this meal reminds the participants of the story of God's provision for His people. Three matzos—pieces of unleavened bread—are included, and one of them is hidden for the children of the family to find. Once it is found, the hidden matzo is broken and eaten. Isn't it interesting that there are three pieces of bread—one each for Father, Son and Holy Spirit? And isn't it interesting that one of them is broken and hidden, just as God the Son was broken and hidden in the grave for three days? Now do Paul's words in 1 Corinthians 11:24 concerning the last supper have more meaning: "This is My body which is broken for you" (NKJV)?

In addition to the bread, the meal includes a plate with several elements. A lamb shank or bone of lamb indicates that the whole Passover lamb was roasted, a method of cooking that was used in the desert, where there was no water for boiling. Bitter herbs (often horseradish today) signified the bitterness of slavery in Egypt. When they would taste the herbs they would wince, remembering their years in bondage as a people of God. Charoset (chopped apples mixed with nuts, sweet wine, honey and cinnamon) symbolized the mortar for the bricks the Israelites were required to make in Egypt. In contrast, parsley reminded them of the sweetness of the promise of God and the new life that comes from God each spring. Today, a roasted egg symbolizes the burning of Jerusalem in AD 70 when the Temple was destroyed. Then a bowl of water with salt was to remind them of the salty tears shed as Hebrew slaves at the hands of their Egyptian taskmasters. Finally, wine was poured to depict the blood of the sacrificed Passover lamb—the lamb that spared their lives and set them free.

That same picture of sacrifice is like a red thread woven through God's whole redemption story. When Adam and Eve sinned in the Garden of Eden, their sin was covered by the slaying of an animal. Prior to the exodus from Egypt, one lamb was sacrificed for each family unit. Then annually, on the Day of Atonement, the priest would go into the holy of holies to sacrifice on behalf of the nation after laying his hands on the head of a goat that he sent out into the wilderness (the "scapegoat" bearing the sins of the people). Finally, at the cross, Jesus sacrificed His life for the entire world: "Look, the Lamb of God, who takes away the sin of the world!" (John 1:29).

This shows His plan of sacrifice first for a man and a woman, then for a family, then for a nation and, ultimately, for the world. "For God so loved the world, that He gave His only begotten Son, that whoever believes in Him should not perish, but have eternal life" (John 3:16, *NASB*). Like a rock hurled into a pond, the ripples of His forgiveness move out in an ever-widening circle. Now each of us, Jew or Gentile, who believes is made righteous before God by the sacrifice, freely given, of Jesus Christ the Lamb of God. On the night of the first Passover, the lamb that was slain spared the Israelites from death; and today, Jesus is our Passover Lamb.

No life worth living is free from sacrifice—chosen sacrifice. There's a difference between sacrifice forced upon you and sacrifice chosen by you. When we willingly choose to sacrifice, our faith grows, because we are saying, "God, You are enough." We grow spiritually when we go without for a deeper reason. I sense the stretching when Kelly and I are at odds, but I stay quiet. I sacrifice the zinger I had ready, because I know God is better. As a father, I'm at my all-time Daddy of high sacrifice when I change "one of those" diapers. Sacrifice is seen throughout the biblical narrative: God sacrificing for us, then calling us to respond; presenting our lives as a living sacrifice (see Rom. 12:1-2). Sacrifice is seen in the Passover meal and then called for from the diners.

God's will requires sacrifice. Sure, there will be blessing; but sacrifice is a part of it. If it doesn't cost you something, it probably isn't done for Him. Does this sacrificial cutting away show an aspect of God that is punishing toward us lowly humans? No, just the opposite. It shows His graciousness to use sacrifice as a tool to strip away our excess baggage. God's great love requires us to lay down our ease. Real life is found in sacrifice, not in acquisition.

God's will requires sacrifice, but miraculously, the sacrifice becomes blessing. For example, the fun of purchasing a new shirt will not even come close to the joy of giving five old ones away. Serving a simple meal at a shelter is better than eating a fancy one at a restaurant. Most of us live in the tension of buying and giving, serving and dining, and that's okay. Both are fine, but lean toward sacrifice. Lean so much that you have to take a step in that direction to regain your footing.

Choosing Sides

After that first memorial meal eaten in haste, with God's people ready to roll, the Egyptians lost their first-born. There was not one Egyptian household without someone dead. It sounds horrible, doesn't it? Before we think, *How cruel of God; how could He?* let us remember that this same Pharaoh is the one who had all of the male Israelite babies thrown into the Nile River soon after their birth—and he's the one who had nine opportunities to repent and give in to the demands of God delivered through Moses. Finally, the tenth-round knockout blow came at midnight, a time symbolic of judgment in Scripture. At the midnight hour, the death angel came, and it was too late for Pharaoh to repent.

There is a time for choosing and a time when choice is no longer possible. C. S. Lewis says it like this, referring to World War II:

> I do not suppose you and I would have thought much of a Frenchman who waited till the Allies were marching into Germany and then announced he was on our side. God will invade. But I wonder whether people who ask God to interfere openly and directly in our world quite

realize what it will be like when He does. When that happens, it is the end of the world. When the author walks on to the stage the play is over. God is going to invade, all right: but what is the good of saying you are on His side then, when you see the whole natural universe melting away like a dream and something else—something it never entered your head to conceive—comes crashing in.[1]

In the judgment of the midnight hour, the death messenger comes as an angel of God, and Pharaoh's options to choose are gone. He has no more time. The author has walked onto the stage, and the play is over. When God invades our world a second time, there will be no more time to deliberate. Lewis continues:

> It will be too late then to choose your side. There is no use saying you choose to lie down when it has become impossible to stand up. That will not be the time for choosing: it will be the time when we discover which side we really have chosen, whether we realized it before or not.[2]

For "at the name of Jesus every knee should bow . . . and every tongue confess that Jesus Christ is Lord" (Phil. 2:10-11). When the midnight hour comes, the question is whether we have already chosen to bow to Christ, or whether we will bow because we can no longer choose to stand.

For those who might wonder about the historicity of the plagues, let me note that the next ruler of Egypt was *not* this pharaoh's firstborn son. We know this because the successor went to great lengths to legitimize his right to the throne, claiming he had had a dream in which the sun god spoke to him and said he would receive the throne. This would not have been necessary if Pharaoh's firstborn son had lived to inherit the throne.

Through the events of the first Passover and the elements of the celebration remembering it, we see that God's will requires sacrifice. We must "paint the door again" in our attitudes and actions, escaping sin's curse of death by trusting the blood of Jesus Christ the Lamb to cover us.

Exchange the Known for the Unknown

As ready as the Israelites must have been to leave slavery in Egypt, they were exchanging 430 years of known history for the unknown wilderness. Leaving was the next logical step after being released by Pharaoh—but to where? When we are unsure of the ultimate destination of God's will, it is enough to simply take the next logical step. I wonder if Todd Beamer or any of his seatmates knew what they would do if they were able to subdue the hijackers and regain control of the plane. I'm guessing none of them were pilots, but they didn't let that concern paralyze them. They simply did the next logical thing and stormed the cockpit.

For Moses and the Israelites, leaving Egypt meant taking a step from the known into the unknown. Have you ever done that? Have you ever driven out of your old driveway and onto the freeway with a U-Haul behind you, moving from the known of a familiar home to the unknown? Students, have you walked through the doors of a new school, not knowing a soul—or into a locker room or onto an athletic field you've never seen before? Ever begun the first day of a new job without a clue about what to do, or perhaps graduated from college and had no idea where your first job might lead you? If so, then you know what a known-to-unknown exodus feels like.

At some point in life, each of us will be faced with a known-to-unknown step in following God's will. The question is whether we will be ready to roll! Are you ready to move from the level of obedience you have known to a new, more challenging level? Ready to move from the comfort of sleeping in on Sundays to become part of a congregation where God desires to use you? Ready to step out from the known of rarely sharing your faith into the wild unknown of flying your flag high for Christ, no matter what "they" might think? Are you ready to roll? Because the truth is, each of us has developed incredible coping mechanisms in our "known" lives. We've developed systems of comfort and ease and efficiency that would very likely disrupt taking the next step. But what if today—right now—God told you to tuck in your robe, get your sandals fastened and be ready to eat and run? Could you? Would you?

Every ready-to-roll heart is powered by the blood of Jesus Christ. The courage to take the next step isn't manufactured through self-effort. It comes from walking by the power of the blood of Jesus Christ into a new covenant, a new relationship. In this new covenant, this new relationship, you will move from the known to the unknown—and when you do, you may just discover the greatest things you have ever discovered in your life!

The Israelites did not leave Egypt alone. God was with them. And they did not leave empty-handed. He provided for them:

> During the night Pharaoh summoned Moses and Aaron and said, "Up! Leave my people, you and the Israelites! Go, worship the LORD as you have requested. Take your flocks and herds, as you have said, and go. And also bless me." The Egyptians urged the people to hurry and leave the country. "For otherwise," they said, "we will all die!" So the people took their dough before the yeast was added, and carried it on their shoulders in kneading troughs wrapped in clothing. The Israelites did as Moses instructed and asked the Egyptians for articles of silver and gold and for clothing (Exod. 12:31-35).

As the Israelites walked out from the known to the unknown, God said, "I'll provide for you." Not only did He provide the blood of lambs to protect them from the death angel, but He also provided plunder from the Egyptians that would sustain them in the desert. And once they were "on the road," He would provide again in the form of manna and quail—their desert diet as they journeyed. Six hundred thousand men plus women and children left Egypt that night—possibly more than 2,000,000 people who were ready to roll!

Finally, It's Time to Roll

It must have seemed to Moses like a long way from a burning bush to a caravan of 2,000,000 Israelites lined up behind him on the road out of Egypt. But Moses simply followed God's will one step at a time. He saw a burning bush. He drew closer to investigate. He focused on pleasing God, not on pleasing the unknown "they." He learned that it is impossible to find God's will without first discovering the God of God's will. And he saw that God's will is always accompanied by God's power. Finally, Moses stepped out of his place of comfort and into a place of challenge, daring to follow God from the known to the unknown. He did the next thing, took the next step in obedience, seeking to know and follow the will of God.

Todd Beamer's rallying call, "Are you guys ready? Let's roll" might not have been familiar to his fellow passengers, but it was a phrase Todd's wife, Lisa, says he used almost every day to shepherd his young children out the door to any family event or outing. On September 11, the words were the same, and the heroism Todd and the others exhibited was for him just the next step in following God's plan for his life. Lisa Beamer put it like this: "On September 11, Todd's mission on earth was complete. He ended daring greatly, not with the cold and timid souls that know neither victory nor defeat (quoting President Roosevelt). Our challenge in this time remaining for us is to each day dare greatly for God, leaving lukewarm faith behind."[3]

Do you hear this widow's brave call to action? She is living out the faith that her husband passed down. It's time for us to leave lukewarm faith behind, too. Are you ready? Through the shed blood of Jesus, the Passover Lamb, you can move out with confidence that God is leading and that His plan will have His power. "Today, if you hear his voice, do not harden your hearts" (Heb. 3:15). Instead, let God hear these words from your heart and your lips: "I am ready, God. Let's roll!"

For Further Reflection and Discussion

1. Are you ready to roll? What's holding you back?

2. How does sacrifice affect your willingness to follow God?

3. If you are in a place of uncertainty, what is the next logical step you might take to know God's will?

4. Is there a time when you have traded the known for the unknown? If so, what was the result?

5. Are you a part of a Bible-teaching church, a community of believers? Why or why not?

Notes
1. C. S. Lewis, *Mere Christianity* (New York: Harper Collins, 1980), p. 65.
2. Ibid.
3. *Reason for Hope* tract (Wheaton, IL: Crossway Books, 2001).

15

IT ALL LEADS TO NOW

July 4, 1776, is a day known in the United States as Independence Day; but do you recall what happened on July 8, 1776? On that day, the freshly signed Declaration of Independence was read publicly for the first time as the Liberty Bell rang in celebration. Moving forward another step in the colonies' quest for freedom from England, a three-man committee of Thomas Jefferson, John Adams and Benjamin Franklin was established to design the great seal of the United States. Mr. Franklin spoke up with the suggestion that the seal and motto that best characterized the spirit of this new nation should include our tour guide of God's will, Moses. His suggested seal pictured Moses lifting up his staff and dividing the Red Sea as Pharaoh and his chariots are washed away by the water. The corresponding motto declared: "Rebellion to tyrants is obedience to God." Thomas Jefferson similarly proposed the seal to be the children of Israel in the wilderness, as a cloud led them by day and pillar of fire by night. What an amazing influence the story of God's will in Moses' life appears to have had on our founding fathers! But somehow Moses lost out to the *e pluribis unum* (Latin for "Out of many, one") motto and an eagle.[1]

The story of the Red Sea crossing is one of the most famous in all of Scripture. Moses and his rag-tag bunch of slaves destroying the well-heeled army of Pharaoh appeals to the heart of anyone rooting for the underdog. This account can encourage us corporately and individually to live the life God intends for us. The Red Sea crossing brings together the many principles we have explored about discovering both God and His will for our journey.

Windshield or Rearview Mirror?

After all that the followers of Moses had seen God do up until this point, you would think their faith would be sky-high. Having witnessed the plagues, seen God's domination of the little-*g* gods of Egypt and Pharaoh's court magicians, they should have been in awe of God, trusting Him with every nuance of life.

They began strong, but their faith didn't last long. Look at the contrast of Exodus 14:8 and 10 (emphasis added):

> The LORD hardened the heart of Pharaoh king of Egypt, so that he pursued the Israelites, *who were marching out boldly* (v. 8).

> As Pharaoh approached, the Israelites looked up, and there were the Egyptians, marching after them. *They were terrified* and cried out to the LORD (v. 10).

Marching boldly in verse 8 . . . terrified in verse 10. I wish we could throw the Israelites under the bus with the other "scaredy cats" of the Bible, but we can relate all too well. Our faith is often just as weak and forgetful. God does so much for us, and we still nervously wonder if He will continue to help. Our passionate "Let's roll!" morphs quickly into "Let's run!" Our moment of boldness becomes a thousand tiny terrors. We are prayed up and desire to share our faith, but when the opportunity arrives, an awkward silence is followed by "How's the weather?" We are enthusiastic about a service opportunity or a new Bible study class, and then never follow through because of the tyranny of the urgent tasks of the day.

What made the change in the celebratory freedmen of Israel? One thing: opposition. When they saw the enemy on their tail, they freaked. The view before them—the windshield—displayed a physical pillar of cloud of God's leadership. But behind them, the rearview mirror showed powerful men in chariots. Which way will you look? Forward or back? "Let's roll" is windshield talk. "Let's run" is rearview mirror talk.

When opposition comes, you are ripe for a miracle if you choose the windshield view of God's leading. Our sandaled friends focused first on the rearview mirror chariots, resulting in complaints and a strange nostalgia for the slavery of the past! They told Moses to leave them alone and wondered aloud if the entire reason for their journey was a shortage of graves in Egypt (see Exod. 14:11-12). Here's the principle at work: When we encounter opposition on the path, the bad ol' days seem like the good ol' days. Slavery is preferable to freedom because slavery is a known commodity. Worry is more familiar than faith, and pride is more natural than humility, so we drift. The old ways and former comrades are recognizable, while trusting God for the new seems lonely and strange.

Fear rarely achieves good results. One writer said, "Fear is the wrong use of imagination. It is anticipating the worst, not the best that can happen."[2] Instead of imagining the worst, think about what will happen when God shows Himself. Dream of the rescue, of what He could do when His hand becomes visible. This is not to set us up for disappointment but to grow our faith by rehearsing miracles in our mind like a child imagining "what if." What if the God who has led us this far really has a plan, and what if that plan is good? What if evil doesn't prevail? What if the Egyptians on one side and the Red Sea on the other are all a part of His plan? What if this is about Him and not about us? What if we don't love our lives even unto death (see Rev. 12:11)? What if God is God?

What if, instead of looking back at Egypt's army in fear, God's people took a cue from their own history and began to focus on the leadership of God up to the critical Red Sea moment. How could the One who had already done so much for them fail them now? Reflect back with me on what we've established so far:

- God's will always has God's power.
- God's will always has God's provision.
- God's will always has God's timing.
- God's will always requires God.
- God's will always matches God's Word.
- God's will always requires obedience and faith.
- God's will always honors God.
- God's will always wins.

The story of God and His people is simply too good to end with the scrolling text: "God failed them and they died . . . The

End." The story is too good; better said, the story is too GOD for that. His plan has to prevail or we've got bigger problems than a few hundred advancing chariots and some horses. We have a failing God.

The same is true for you. God is weaving a story of His power in your life. He won't fail you. The Lord is batting a thousand in the category of faithfulness. Contrary to others' opinions or your fears, you aren't about to be His first "oops." As Chuck Swindoll encourages, "God has never missed a runway through all the centuries of fearful fog."[3]

Parked-Car Conversations

It seems like meaningful conversations often happen in parked cars. The chatter goes deeper as they drive, then two friends arrive, and sit in the car to continue the discussion. I see this happen with my wife and a friend of hers. They go to a Living Proof Bible Study led by Beth Moore at our church each Tuesday night. Without fail, the car pulls into our driveway to drop Kelly off and it sits there, running, for another 30 minutes. As these two ladies talk, they probably use more gas in our driveway than on the trip to and from the church. But the conversation's sweetness is rich after a wonderful time of Bible study together, so they linger and continue to chat.

I've had my share of parked-car conversations with friends too. One in particular took place at a time when I was feeling discouraged. Life seemed like a cliff that was growing higher and higher while I clung to its edge. The growing responsibilities of each day were easy to measure, but was my personal growth keeping the same pace? I explained my situation to my friend, using aeronautical terms, comparing myself to an exhilarated stunt pilot performing a barrel roll in an air show. What fun at first, what a dream! But there was also a fear that the exhilarating barrel roll could become a nosedive at any second. I was even a bit worried that God might become the sabotage agent of my flight, just to "teach me something."

My wise friend reminded me of all that God had already done in my life to bring me such a long, long way. Why would He now be my downfall? My friend also reminded me of God's provision. "Gregg," he said, "the story is too good so far; He's not going to fail you now." I truly needed to hear that. A parked-car conversation with a friend can keep you on the path.

If we're going to look backward, we need to look back at Him. Reflecting back on all that God has done strengthens our faith that He is able to take us on the next step. Our faith is weak and forgetful, so we need to remember that He is leading us day and night. He can be trusted more than the familiar things of our past or the frightening things in our future. Radical faith will take us farther than irrational fear; fear paralyzes, but faith energizes.

Irrational fear can strike anyone, anywhere . . . even the president in the White House. When President Benjamin Harrison was in office during the late 1800s, a newfangled convenience was installed at 1600 Pennsylvania Avenue: electricity. President and Mrs. Harrison were so intimidated by the invention that we consider normal and indispensable, they would not touch the switches to operate the lights. Many a night they slept with the lights on because there was not a housekeeper close by to flip the switch. Process this story for a moment. The leader of the free world was afraid to flip a light switch! We look back on that with a laugh, knowing from our perspective that his fear was irrational. But at the time it must have surely seemed real.[4]

So it goes with God's will. The army of your enemy may seem numerous, and the sea may look deep, but we've seen God's hand. Let the work of the Lord in your past compel you in the present. Take the next step forward in faith. Even if your feet get wet in the sea, He'll split the waves at the exact moment necessary. God's will always has God's power and His timing. He is telling a story with your life that shines with His glory, not your own. It is His name on the line, not yours—and He always protects His name.

Picture the stage set for another showdown of faith between God and Pharaoh, with Moses as God's chosen leader. The venue has changed from the boxing ring of the plagues to a place by the sea. Pharaoh's army is chasing down the free men of God. They have no place to go. The sea is in front of them and a mighty army is in back. It is time for God to show up, and He does, in a BIG way.

God's Will Brings Unexpected Paths

Moses, as he was raised in the spectacular rooms of Pharaoh's palace, could never have perceived the strange direction his life would take. The deliverer from the tyranny of Pharaoh had once called him friend. What irony! Many paths of life are unexpected, to say the least. As a word of caution, truly following Christ will result in more unexpected turns than expected ones.

The surrendering of our will and dreams to the Lord puts us on the highway but not behind the wheel.

God's unexpected paths far exceed our shortsighted expectations. With water before them and an army pressing in behind, the children of Israel seemed out of good choices. Think of all the ways that God could have intervened in this situation. The Israelites could have turned to fight back the army. This was the strategy God used with Gideon; small army beats big army. The Lord could have turned Pharaoh's militia around with a vision of angels surrounding them as He did with Elisha. Stones from the water's edge slung in David vs. Goliath style could have done the trick, or if the water had to be included, why not a preview of Peter's stroll on top? Instead, the unthinkable and the unexpected way opens up. What would happen if God . . . split the sea in two?!

> Then Moses stretched out his hand over the sea, and all that night the LORD drove the sea back with a strong east wind and turned it into dry land. The waters were divided, and the Israelites went through the sea on dry ground, with a wall of water on their right and on their left (Exod. 14:21-22).

WOW! Unexpected is how God rolls. When you are trapped at the water's edge, keep walking, because God opens unexpected paths. With this kind of miracle, the power, timing and leadership are entirely the Lord's. What a walk of faith to stroll between two walls of water, thought to be at least 20 feet high! The Hebrew word used for "wall" connotes a massively large (usually a city) wall.[5] Each step they took could be their last as the deafening water roared to the right and left. Faith in an unexpected path, trusting the impossible, is reality.

Hudson Taylor, the nineteenth-century British missionary to China, vowed, "I have found that there are three stages to every great work of God: first, it is impossible, then it is difficult, then it is done."[6] What does that mean for you today? What army and sea do you sense moving in? God will do something unexpected. A path of clearing and guidance will come from an unexpected but miraculous place. Stay faithful, roll up your jeans and walk through the water when He splits it apart.

All Your Steps Lead to the Next One

God has been growing the faith of Moses step by step for years to get to this beach. Often we look way out on the horizon and declare, "I could never do that." One day God may want you to do "that," but God wants you to do "this" first. Take the first step before you today and you'll be ready for the next step necessary tomorrow. Life is not a prepackaged item purchased from the middle shelf; it is a basket filled with something from every aisle.

One day, I asked a father of four how he managed to care for such an active family. His response gives clarity to our point. He said, "You don't have them all at once. It comes slowly, and you transition with each one." Similarly, Moses didn't go from lifting the staff of a sheep shepherd to lifting the staff of a sea-splitter in a single day. Even Moses was in the process of growing faith.

- He saw a bush that wouldn't burn up.
- He heard God's call.
- He had to be taught that arguing with God doesn't work.
- With Aaron by his side, he walked into Pharaoh's court with a demand.
- He witnessed God's power through the plagues.

Finally, walking out of town wearing a "mission accomplished" button on his tunic, he reaches the water's edge in a deadly predicament. After all of the faith-building of the previous miracles, then after all the prayers, then after discovering the God of his call . . . he walks through the sea on dry land! As the proverb states, "The man who says it can't be done should not interrupt the man who is doing it."

The path of God's will for your life is the same. Yesterday prepared you for today. So don't stay stalled at yesterday's faith; take the next step. Plateaus are not God's will for anyone. Get out of the mud. Step faithfully one more time. What is your next step? In the Exodus, the next step was literally onto the sea bottom.

Of course, the thick-skulled Pharaoh pursued.

It is unbelievable that he hadn't gotten the message. But at the same time, how many times have we continued to pursue our plans when God has been powerfully and consistently directing us elsewhere? Our quests result in confusion. While God's bushes never burn up, ours ultimately do. Only His will lasts for the long term. Even if your own chariot takes you 50 years through the sea, its wheels will ultimately fail.

During the *last watch* of the night the LORD looked down from the pillar of fire and cloud at the Egyptian army and threw it into *confusion*. He made the *wheels of their chariots come off* so that they had difficulty driving. And the Egyptians said, "Let's get away from the Israelites! The LORD is fighting for them against Egypt" (Exod. 14:24-25, emphasis added).

The checklist of gear, skill and education is slanted completely in favor of the pursuing Egyptian army, but life, faith and God's will belong to His people. Therefore, the victory is God's. Moses and his followers stood on the opposite shore as their pursuers died in the sea. God's will always wins.

Closing and Continuing

We've been on quite a journey through the chapters of this book. By looking at the beginning steps of the Exodus, we have taken some principles for our own life. The journey is not only to discover God's will for our lives, but to also discover the God of God's will. Our search strategically concludes at the crossing of the Red Sea. But there is much more to the life of Moses: still ahead are the Ten Commandments, the golden calf, manna, water from a rock and many peaks and valleys. Keep reading the book of Exodus and look for God's hand at work all the way.

There is also much more to your life ahead. We've stopped mid-sea in the life of Moses to symbolically say that your life is continuing on as well. God willing, you have years ahead of you, with a thousand forks in the road. Keep walking in faith and trusting His whispers of direction. He will lead you as He did Moses. It won't be with a pillar of cloud or fire, but there will be a voice, still and small but effective. To hear from God and shout, "Yes!" is the joy of life. Christ's great power in you comes alive as God's will unfolds before you. What a thought that a shepherd, in the middle of nowhere, with a felony to his account, could become the Moses we remember now by simply and consistently saying yes.

God's desire to take a person from "wandering" to "called" still exists today. He wants to take people who feel useless and make them known for their usefulness. He can steer a person from a string of poor decisions to being revered as wise beyond their years. Jesus is a straight-A student in the class of life-change and has every PhD possible in leadership. Daily, we must embrace the guidance of the Lord. Only then will the wonderful combination of knowing God and knowing His will come together synergistically. Make it your ambition, make it your aspiration to know Christ; then His will becomes the natural result. Seek first His kingdom and righteousness and all these things will be added unto you (see Matt. 6:33).

Go, friend, go! Find God's will. Seek Him, know Him, take the next step.

That day the LORD saved Israel from the hands of the Egyptians, and Israel saw the Egyptians lying dead on the shore. And when the Israelites saw the great power the LORD displayed against the Egyptians, *the people feared the LORD and put their trust in him and in Moses his servant* (Exod. 14:30-31, emphasis added).

For Further Reflection and Discussion

1. What is the next step for you in the journey of discovering God's will?
2. How has He been preparing you for this step?
3. What was your primary "aha!" moment as you read this book, and what is its primary application in your life?

Notes

1. William J. Federer, *Great Quotations* (St. Louis, MO: Amerisearch; 2001).
2. Cited in James S. Hewett, ed., *Illustrations Unlimited* (Carol Stream, IL: Tyndale, 1988), p. 205.
3. Chuck Swindoll, *Growing Strong in the Seasons of Life* (Grand Rapids, MI: Zondervan, 1983).
4. "Benjamin Harrison," *New Word Enclyclopedia,* April 3, 2008. http://www.newworlden cyclopedia.org/entry/Benjamin_Harrison.
5. Douglas Stuart, *Exodus: The Electronic Edition,* Logos Library System, *New American Commentary II* (Nashville, TN: Broadman and Holman Publishers, 2007), s. 36.
6. Nick Harrison, *The Magnificent Prayer* (Grand Rapids, MI: Zondervan, 2001), p. 428.

Forty Verses from God's Word on God's Will

Throughout this book we have sought to establish the importance of the Bible in discovering God's will, and the God of God's will. Without the blueprint of the Bible our lives can't be built upon a secure foundation. What follows are verses of Scripture to help you on your journey from the bushing-bush to the Red Sea and beyond. Here are a few ideas of how these verses can be used:

- Read through them for encouragement.
- Select a few to commit to memory (maybe with your kids, spouse or a friend).
- Tear this list out of the book and tuck it into your Bible. (It is okay to rip the pages out; you bought the book! If you borrowed it, then don't rip out the pages.)
- Write a favorite verse on a note card and tape it to your mirror.
- But for sure, believe them, live them and put them into action.

Living It Out

"Should you then seek great things for yourself? Seek them not" (Jer. 45:5).

"Whoever does God's will is my brother and sister and mother" (Mark 3:35).

"For my Father's will is that everyone who looks to the Son and believes in him should have eternal life, and I will raise him up at the last day" (John 6:40).

"Jesus answered, 'My teaching is not my own. It comes from him who sent me. If anyone chooses to do God's will, he will find out whether my teaching comes from God or whether I speak on my own'" (John 7:16-17).

"Therefore, I urge you, brothers, in view of God's mercy, to offer your bodies as living sacrifices, holy and pleasing to God—this is your spiritual act of worship. Do not conform any longer to the pattern of this world, but be transformed by the renewing of your mind. Then you will be able to test and approve what God's will is—his good, pleasing and perfect will" (Rom. 12:1-2).

"He predestined us to be adopted as his sons through Jesus Christ, in accordance with his pleasure and will—to the praise of his glorious grace, which he has freely given us in the One he loves" (Eph. 1:5-6).

"Be very careful, then, how you live—not as unwise but as wise, making the most of every opportunity, because the days are evil. Therefore do not be foolish, but understand what the Lord's will is. Do not get drunk on wine, which leads to debauchery. Instead, be filled with the Spirit" (Eph. 5:15-18).

"It is God who is at work in you to will and to act according to his good purpose" (Phil. 2:13).

"For this reason, since the day we heard about you, we have not stopped praying for you and asking God to fill you with the knowledge of his will through all spiritual wisdom and understanding" (Col. 1:9).

"Epaphras, who is one of you and a servant of Christ Jesus, sends greetings. He is always wrestling in prayer for you, that you may stand firm in all the will of God, mature and fully assured" (Col. 4:12).

"It is God's will that you should be sanctified: that you should avoid sexual immorality; that each of you should learn to control his own body in a way that is holy and honorable, not in passionate lust like the heathen, who do not know God; and that in this matter no one should wrong his brother or take advantage of him" (1 Thess. 4:3-6).

"Be joyful always; pray continually; give thanks in all circumstances, for this is God's will for you in Christ Jesus" (1 Thess. 5:16-18).

"But just as he who called you is holy, so be holy in all you do; for it is written: 'Be holy, because I am holy'" (1 Pet. 1:15-16).

Suffering

"For it is God's will that by doing good you should silence the ignorant talk of foolish men" (1 Pet. 2:15).

"It is better, if it is God's will, to suffer for doing good than for doing evil" (1 Pet. 3:17).

"So then, those who suffer according to God's will should commit themselves to their faithful Creator and continue to do good" (1 Pet. 4:19).

God's Guidance

"Look to the LORD and his strength; seek his face always" (1 Chron. 16:11).

"He guides the humble in what is right and teaches them his way" (Ps. 25:9).

"Who, then, is the man that fears the LORD? He will instruct him in the way chosen for him" (Ps. 25:12).

"Since you are my rock and my fortress, for the sake of your name lead and guide me" (Ps. 31:3).

"I will instruct you and teach you in the way you should go; I will counsel you and watch over you" (Ps. 32:8).

"Delight yourself in the LORD and he will give you the desires of your heart" (Ps. 37:4).

"Be still before the LORD and wait patiently for him; do not fret when men succeed in their ways, when they carry out their wicked schemes" (Ps. 37:7).

"For this God is our God for ever and ever; he will be our guide even to the end" (Ps. 48:14).

"You guide me with your counsel, and afterward you will take me into glory" (Ps. 73:24).

"Your word is a lamp to my feet and a light for my path" (Ps. 119:105).

"But whoever listens to me will live in safety, and be at ease, without fear of harm" (Prov. 1:33).

"For the LORD gives wisdom, and from his mouth come knowledge and understanding. He holds victory in store for the upright, he is a shield to those whose walk is blameless, for he guards the course of the just and protects the way of his faithful ones. Then you will understand what is right and just and fair—every good path" (Prov. 2:6-9).

"Trust in the LORD with all your heart and lean not on your own understanding; in all your ways acknowledge him, and he will make your paths straight" (Prov. 3:5-6).

"When you walk, [God's commands] will guide you; when you sleep, they will watch over you; when you awake, they will speak to you" (Prov. 6:22).

"The integrity of the upright guides them, but the unfaithful are destroyed by their duplicity" (Prov. 11:3).

"Plans fail for lack of counsel, but with many advisers they succeed" (Prov. 15:22).

"In his heart a man plans his course, but the LORD determines his steps" (Prov. 16:9).

"Whether you turn to the right or to the left, your ears will hear a voice behind you, saying, 'This is the way; walk in it'" (Isa. 30:21).

"This is what the LORD says—your Redeemer, the Holy One of Israel: 'I am the LORD your God, who teaches you what is best for you, who directs you in the way you should go'" (Isa. 48:17).

"I know, O LORD, that a man's life is not his own; it is not for man to direct his steps" (Jer. 10:23).

"'For I know the plans I have for you,' declares the LORD, 'plans to prosper you and not to harm you, plans to give you hope and a future. Then you will call upon me and come and pray to me, and I will listen to you. You will seek me and find me when you seek me with all your heart'" (Jer. 29:11-13).

"Call to me and I will answer you and tell you great and unsearchable things you do not know" (Jer. 33:3).

"Seek first his kingdom and his righteousness, and all these things will be given to you as well" (Matt. 6:33).

"So I say to you: Ask and it will be given to you; seek and you will find; knock and the door will be opened to you. For everyone who asks receives; he who seeks finds; and to him who knocks, the door will be opened" (Luke 11:9-10).

Forty Great Quotes on God's Will

1. "Let God's promises shine on your problems." (Corrie ten Boom)
2. "There are two kinds of people: those who say to God, 'Thy will be done,' and those to whom God says, 'All right, then, have it your way.'" (C. S. Lewis)
3. "Every evening I turn my worries over to God. He's going to be up all night anyway." (Mary C. Crowley)
4. "A man with God is always in the majority." (John Knox)
5. "God's will is not an itinerary, but an attitude." (Andrew Dhuse)
6. "Be God or let God." (Author unknown)
7. "Most people wish to serve God—but only in an advisory capacity." (Author unknown)
8. "Availability is better than ability for God." (Author unknown)
9. "If you are not as close to God as you used to be, who moved?" (Author unknown)
10. "We're not necessarily doubting that God will do the best for us; we are wondering how painful the best will turn out to be." (C. S. Lewis)
11. "The will of God will never take you to where the grace of God will not protect you." (Author unknown)

12. "Only he who believes is obedient, and only he who is obedient believes." (Dietrich Bonhoeffer)

13. "Earthly possessions dazzle our eyes and delude us into thinking that they can provide security and freedom from anxiety. Yet all the time they are the very source of all anxiety." (Dietrich Bonhoeffer)

14. "One man or woman called to God is worth a hundred who have elected to work for God." (Oswald Chambers)

15. "Have you ever thought that our disappointments are God's way of reminding us that there are idols in our lives that must be dealt with?" (Erwin Lutzer)

16. "I have always felt that although someone may defeat me, and I strike out in a ball game, the pitcher on the particular day was the best player. But I know when I see him again, I'm going to be ready for his curve ball. Failure is a part of success." (Hank Aaron)

17. "We failed, but in the good providence of God apparent failure often proves a blessing." (Robert E. Lee)

18. "I honestly think it is better to be a failure at something you love than to be a success at something you hate." (George Burns)

19. "It is better to fail in a cause that will ultimately succeed, than to succeed in a cause that will ultimately fail." (Peter Marshall)

20. "Success is living in such a way that you are using what God has given you—your intellect, abilities, and energy—to reach the purpose that he intends for your life." (Kathi Hudson)

21. "How free you are when you do all things simply to the glory of God. There is nothing simpler or more faithful than learning to accept the will of God apart from your personal taste—your likes and dislikes and impulses." (François Fénelon)

22. "When God gives a command or a vision of truth, it is never a question of what He will do but of what we will do. To be successful in God's work is to fall in line with His will and to do it His way. All that is pleasing to Him is a success." (Henrietta Mears)

23. "Expect great things from God; attempt great things for God." (William Carey)

24. "If you read history, you will find that the Christians who did most for the present world were just those who thought most of the next. . . . Aim at heaven and you will get earth 'thrown in'; aim at earth and you will get neither." (C. S. Lewis)

25. "A man's heart is right when he wills what God wills." (Thomas Aquinas)

26. "God's work done in God's way will never lack God's supply." (Hudson Taylor)

27. "The pessimist complains about the wind. The optimist expects it to change. The leader adjusts the sails." (John C. Maxwell)

28. "By perseverance, the snail reached the ark." (Charles H. Spurgeon)

29. "Rebellion against God does not begin with the clenched fist of atheism but with the self-satisfied heart of the one for whom 'thank you' is redundant." (Os Guinness)

30. "God made us: invented us as man made the engine. A car is made to run on gasoline, and it would not run properly on anything else. Now God designed the human machine to run on Himself. He Himself is the fuel our spirits were designed to feed on. There is no other. That is why it is just no good asking God to make us happy in our own way without bothering about religion. God cannot give us a happiness apart from Himself, because it is not there. There is no such thing." (C. S. Lewis)

31. "When told there was only 25 cents in the China Inland Mission's bank account, Hudson Taylor said, 'Praise God, 25 cents plus all the promises of God!'"

32. "The maid who sweeps her kitchen is doing the will of God just as much as the monk who prays. Not because she may sing a Christian hymn as she sweeps but because God loves clean floors. The Christian shoemaker does his Christian duty not by putting little crosses on the shoes, but by making good shoes, because God is interested in good craftsmanship." (Martin Luther)

33. "God is not a cosmic bellboy for whom we can press a button to get things done." (Harry Emerson Fosdick)

34. "How idle it is to call certain things God-sends! As if there was anything else in the world." (Augustus William Hare and Julius Charles Hare)

35. "Remember this. When people choose to withdraw far from a fire, the fire continues to give warmth, but they grow cold. When people choose to withdraw far from light, the light continues to be bright in itself but they are in darkness. This is also the case when people withdraw from God." (Augustine)

36. "We need not fear shipwreck when God is the pilot." (Henry Ward Beecher)

37. "Your mind works very simply: you are either trying to find out what are God's laws in order to follow them; or you are trying to outsmart Him." (Martin H. Fischer)

38. "God often visits us, but most of the time we are not at home." (Joseph Roux)

39. "I would rather walk with God in the dark than go alone in the light." (Mary Gardiner Brainard)

40. "Once you find God and give your heart to Him, His will finds you." (Tony Evans)

SEVEN QUESTIONS TO DETERMINE GOD'S WILL

1. What does the Bible say about the issue?

2. What does a wise, trusted Christian in your life think you should do?

3. Does this fit your spiritual giftedness and passions?

4. What do you want to do?

5. What do you sense God leading you to do?

6. What doors have opened or closed?

7. Which path requires more faith and could bring God the greatest glory?

ABOUT CAMP AMAZON

A ski trip that was meant to bond a group involved in a discipleship program at T Bar M left director Keith Myer with an unsatisfying void in his program. That dissatisfaction led T Bar M to the mission field, and the program took flight in 1998, with an outback trip to the mountains of Panama. It was then that God gave roots to a Mission Adventure Program with T Bar M's desire to use sports as a vehicle to spread God's love outside their camp gates.

More than 20 trips later, T Bar M decided to take their mission efforts to the next level and created T Bar M Camps Around the World. The plan involved a three-year effort to partner with a local missionary, purchase land, build facilities and train a staff to run a Christ-centered adventure camp. The goal was to have the property sustaining itself within a three-year period in order to leave the camp in local hands. In 2006, T Bar M partnered with Abundant Life Ministries in Iquitos, Peru, for its first ground-zero project called Camp Amazon. In 2009, Camp Amazon held seven weeks of camp, bringing almost 600 children to hear about Christ in a camp atmosphere for the first time. A second season was completed in 2010 with 20 local staff running all aspects of camp with limited oversight by T Bar M.

If you are interested in learning more about Camp Amazon or T Bar M's Mission Adventure Program, you can go to www.TBarMCamps.org.

Thanks for your purchase of this book! A portion of the author's royalties will go to help Camp Amazon.

ABOUT THE AUTHOR

Gregg Matte was born and raised in Houston, Texas, and trusted Christ as his Savior at the age of 16. Since then, God has done a tremendous work in him and through him. In 1989, as a Texas A&M sophomore, Gregg and his roommates started a small Bible study named Breakaway in their apartment. Under Gregg's leadership, Breakaway exploded, reaching more than 4,000 students each week. In 2004, God called Gregg to become the pastor of Houston's First Baptist Church. Today, this great church has grown tremendously and is impacting the world as never before. Gregg holds a marketing degree from Texas A&M and a master's degree in Christian Education from Southwestern Baptist Theological Seminary. Most importantly, Gregg is married to Kelly and is a father of two: Greyson and Valerie.

Contact Gregg Matte at
pastorgregg@houstonsfirst.org

Check out his website at
www.houstonsfirst.org
www.greggmatte.com